THE GOD-MIND CONNECTION

As Revealed Through
Jean K. Foster

Request for such permission should be addressed to:

Uni★Sun
P.O. Box 25421
Kansas City, MO 64119

This book is manufactured in the United States of America. Cover art by Bradley Dehner and distribution by Stillpoint Publishing.

Stillpoint Publishing
Box 640, Meetinghouse Road
Walpole, NH 03608

Publishing simultaneously in Canada
by Fitzhenry and Whiteside Limited, Toronto.

ISBN # 0-913299-37-5

A JOINT
Uni★Sun / Stillpoint
BOOK

THE GOD-MIND CONNECTION
As revealed to Jean K. Foster

CHAPTER 1—Receiving Counsel from the
Brotherhood of God. 1

Spirit counselors, who call themselves the "Brotherhood,"
open up the lines of communication with the author.

CHAPTER 2—Forming a Partnership. 9

How we can form a partnership with the Brotherhood of
God and receive the help they have for each of us. The
Brotherhood gives only good gifts to those who team up
with them.

CHAPTER 3—Growing into the Person You Want To Be. . . . 15

All of us can become exactly what we want to be—with
the help of the Brotherhood and by way of the plan of
reincarnation. One lifetime is never enough to grow into
the person we want to be.

Chapter 4—Considering the God of the Universe 21

How to widen our concept of God by taking away all the
limitations we now practice—even those given by
churches, those given by Bible interpreters, and those
presented by evangelists.

CHAPTER 5—Walking into the Bright Sun of God 27

The author's personal growth experience that came from
the counseling by the Brotherhood is detailed here. Her
concept of Jesus changed; her belief in reincarnation was
strengthened, and revelations about "dead" friends were
given.

CHAPTER 6—Finding the Way to Truth 37

There is a way to discover truth, but churches may not be the answer. Truth comes directly to individuals, not through institutions.

CHAPTER 7—Learning more about the next Plane of Life. . 47

Learn to express our thoughts into things, not only on the next plane of life, but in this earth plane too. The quality of life on the next plane depends on our ability to use thought effectively to produce what is good.

CHAPTER 8—Working out Our Destiny 59

Manifesting our dreams, working with our own truth in making decisions, emptying our ego so God may fill us, giving up our bodies to advanced souls, opening our eyes to universal truth.

CHAPTER 9—Standing on the Promises of God. 71

Twenty-three promises of God. What they are and how to collect on them.

CHAPTER 10—Losing our Identities and
Finding Them Again 79

A history of the spirit-entities who separated from God. We have the freedom to choose God or to reject Him.

CHAPTER 11—Crying in the Wilderness. 87

The Brotherhood explains the difference between "earth-mind" and "God-mind." They present the picture of people who want the best in their lives, but who accept the least because they listen to the wrong mind.

CHAPTER 12—Progressing Spirits—Stories about the
Brotherhood 101

These lifetime after lifetime stories of the Brotherhood show their failures, their progression, their eventual growth into the advanced souls who counsel us from the next plane of life.

CHAPTER 13—Receiving the Truth from God-Mind 115

The Brotherhood explains how correspondence takes place between them and the writer. It is told strictly from their point of view along with a step by step process that others may use.

CHAPTER 14—Teaming Up With
the Brotherhood of God................ 125

The Brotherhood recalls the key points of this book and reveals the way in which the reader and the Brotherhood may unite to enjoy a rich, satisfying counseling service.

FOREWORD

When my wife first asked me to write the foreword to this book, I was pretty flip with my response. After all, how many husbands are invited to write the foreword to books written by their wives?

Then I read the first chapter. And the second chapter. I had so many questions, my wife told me to skip the rest of the book and jump to Chapter 13. What I read there was even more startling, so I read the entire book. What I learned was that the mother of my children, a college graduate, professional teacher, and occasional writer of articles for a wide variety of church publications, believes that she is:

a) Communicating with people from another world,

b) Receiving instructions, via her typewriter, from "spirit counselors,"

c) Learning about reincarnation from the "Brotherhood," and

d) Receiving instructions on living from a plane above our earthly plane which will enable her to live a better life now.

She also told me that she isn't the girl I married on the campus of Indiana University 37 years ago. I didn't realize what she meant until I read about the "re-entry of souls" in Chapter 8.

I've never known my wife to lie, and she avoids controversy and/or confrontations (and this book will undoubtedly create both). In short, there is no doubt in my mind that she believes everything she has written in this book.

In retrospect, I also know that she has startled me on several occasions with "revelations" of her "conversations" with people who have died. Up to the time she started on this book, it was easier for me, her husband, to simply change the subject.

In discussions with Jean, I find her firm in her belief that her purpose in writing the book is to emphasize a Universal God who can help people in their daily lives.

From my viewpoint, the awesome part of the book is how she gathered the material.

There will be those skeptics who, if they even read the book in its entirety, will say that Jean wrote the book out of her own life experiences—plus a vivid imagination. But I also read the first draft of Chapter 13, and then most of the other chapters, from her original notes. It is not her writing. She couldn't have written that much on that subject in that length of time without outside help.

Once I came to the conclusion that she really did receive direction in her writing, it became easier for me to accept the fact that the entire book is the result of her communication with spirits who are on a different plane than mortals on earth.

Also, if I could accept the fact that the writing (inspiration) came to her through a thought transfer from outside sources, then it was relatively easy to accept the premise that there is another, second plane of life. Furthermore, there is a Brotherhood which can and does communicate with people on earth, and they are good spirits, dedicated to helping people on earth. If Jean, who is not clairvoyant can do it, then anyone—with a little practice—can do it.

It follows that it is also reasonable to accept the message of Jean's book that there is a Universal God and that there are spiritual counselors who are readily available to help anyone attain a happy, successful life on earth.

Carl B. Foster

CHAPTER 1

RECEIVING COUNSEL
FROM THE BROTHERHOOD OF GOD

How will counsel from the Brotherhood affect my life?

"If people will turn their attention to us, give us their open minds, their open hearts, then we will fill them with wisdom and with the gifts of spirit that will bring them into oneness with God. This is our task here—to take the God-message to you on your plane that you will not waste your life there."

Thus began one of many morning sessions at my typewriter. The hands on the keys of my typewriter were mine, but the impetus to strike certain letters came from an unseen source. Later I was to learn that the source is a God-created group of spirit entities called the Brotherhood of God, the Counselor that Jesus promised.

Automatic writing—as many call it—is not automatic according to those in the Brotherhood. "It comes with practice on your part and with the power of God working in us both."

My experiment to contact someone in the next plane of life began with pencil and paper and a willingness to find out for myself if I could do this kind of writing. In the next chapter I explain my step-by-step progression from swirls and figure eights to the typing I do now. In Chapter 13 a messenger from the Brotherhood explains in much detail how the system works.

The message that came to me day by day, I soon learned, was not intended for me alone. This enlightenment was for everyone. "You are to write a book," my communicator told me. I protested ignorance of the subject, no experience in religious books, no prestigious publishing history. But my assignment grew into reality as a wealth of information and counsel appeared on my typewritten page.

"This book is to be about growth," one of the Brothers told me. "Growth is the goal of your life. Be open to this thought. Be open to growth. No one can just ride along in life without something happening. Either a person grows or a person goes into decline. No one stays the same. There is no use in trying to hide from this truth. When you finish with your body, you come here to this second level of life, to this plane that looks so much like the earth plane. It is here you rest and contemplate your earth life and then go on with your true life.

"If you decline in your earth life instead of growing, you must go through growth here on this plane. But it is much harder here because there is no hardship to go through or overcome. There is no lesson to learn through living. The Brotherhood of God is here to help, to counsel, but not to direct. We transfer spiritual gifts to you, but we do not act in your place. You must act. We must help. That is our relationship."

The Bible has references to the Counselor that Jesus promised. Two of these are in the book of John, the 14th chapter. The first reference from my Revised Standard Version, the 16th verse, gives Jesus' words: "And I will pray the Father, and He will give you another Counselor, to be with you forever. . . ." And in the 26th verse Jesus says, "But the Counselor, the Holy Spirit, whom the Father will send in my name, he will teach you all things, and bring to your remembrance all that I have said to you."

"By having the Brotherhood span both planes," my communicator said, "it can work effectively with you." I asked what they meant by "their plane," and here is the response. "This plane is with yours—on the entering level of the next part of life. We are not far. This plane is so near you that your breath is felt here. This plane is the image of yours except that it is more perfect. This plane has the hopes and dreams of man expressed in many ways. The ecology is perfect."

Those advanced spirits insisted that we are to call upon their help in all things affecting our growth. They define growth as that which gives us the power to be one with God. "The energy of the God of the Universe is open to people on both planes. It comes through the Brotherhood of God to help you to become the person you want to be."

Two questions came to mind. First, what is meant by "the energy of the God of the Universe?" And second, is the person we want to be the same as being one with God?

"Energy is the power of God on the move throughout the universe. This energy gives you the power to turn thoughts into things. This energy, remember, is of God, not the Brotherhood. We only open your mind to its presence here. We give you the open channel—the means to open your mind to receive this energy.

"It is the spiritual law that we want to become one with God. This desire is written into our eternal plan. This is the plan of the spirit since before the earth began."

Now back to that part about energy, or "the power of God on the move." What did my communicator mean by energy that turns thought into things?

"This energy will be your price of things. Like money is the price of things on your plane, this energy is the price of things here, but not only here, on your plane too."

Could these Brothers be talking literally here? Can we turn thoughts into things by use of this special energy?

"You become the proper channel on the use of this power and you manifest what you desire."

Surely there must be a misunderstanding! Things are material. Surely this message means that we manifest qualities like goodness or peacefulness.

Like any good and patient teacher, the messenger from the Brotherhood continued. "You can manifest qualities, of course, but you can also manifest things." Again I protested, shaking my head in contradiction. But this Brother persisted. "You can manifest what you desire by using this power or energy that is available to you now. Be open. Be ready."

Astonished by the idea of demonstrating this power in a material way, I asked how I might receive this energy. Thereupon I received a spiritual blueprint that anyone can use to manifest the good in life.

"This is the method: Be open to us here. Keep your mind turned toward your good, your spiritual good. Then if your desire is in line with that spiritual good, it will manifest." And who decides about our spiritual good? "Spiritual good to one is not spiritual good to another. Turn your thoughts to us here to have this matter enlightened."

Still, I resisted the idea of manifesting things. "Why," I asked, "do I resist this idea?"

"Because you have been taught differently. Because you keep believing that there is a difference between spiritual life and the one in which you manifest material things. It is all the same. It is not separate. Be open. Say good-by to your negative thoughts. This is not the time for weakness. It is a time for strength. You have a goal in mind, don't you? Then manifest success by the use of the energy that is here for you, this power."

"Today is the day," the communicator continued. "Be open in this matter. You seek success. You want to demonstrate this success in money. You want satisfaction. You want confidence in yourself. You desire these last two above all material things. Then put this on the map of your imagination. See it happening. Be open to success. Plan your use of success. Be on this matter in prayer. Imprint it on your inner eye. The power comes in to you to make it manifest. We in the Brotherhood are open toward this accomplishment. It is certainly in line with your spiritual good. It is a right desire. It is God at work within you to help you carry out your plan of becoming the person you want to be."

At this point I took one of my favorite articles from my rejected manuscripts, worked it over again, and sent it out. It seemed a time for action, for a step of faith in the Brotherhood's words.

"How can we know," I asked, "what our spiritual good is?"

"The Brotherhood is always here on this plane, open to your plane. Your thought sent to us will bring you the help you seek. Prayer is to God—that which gives you the oneness with Him. But when you think that you want us in your life helping, counseling, giving good gifts, we will turn ourselves toward you in the open channel to contact your mind. Be open. Go to the God you already know, and think of the help you need."

I asked for enlightenment on the kind of help we might ask for. "The Brotherhood will help people think more clearly about what life is for, what purpose each one has. We care that you become the best that you can be. People can overcome depression and loneliness because they know there are friends here as well as there, and no person goes his way alone.

"God is the reality one hopes for when you turn to the Brotherhood for help. But 'help' is perhaps not the word we need here. 'Help' concentrates us on need, and many people would rather do things on their own. A better word might be *growth*, for most want to be spirits that grow, right? It's a more positive picture. This group of advanced spirits exists that growth may progress on the earth plane in great strides. The work we do is to point the way to God-life in each person. God is the God of us all."

"And you always come when thought is turned toward you?" I asked.

"This Brotherhood is open on this side all the time. We want to help. We want to bring you the gifts of spirit that God has in your name. Each person has the gifts here, and we help to transfer these to the willing open individual."

"Can everyone make contact with you?" I asked my communicator.

"I tell you the truth, that everyone who wishes to be open to the Brotherhood of God can be so. This is not difficult to do. It is only a matter of will and of desire on the part of anyone. You only think it's difficult because it isn't common yet, but communication is the part that is best between you and us. We can become helpful to you in your growth there because we can unite with you. Think on this matter carefully: *People may be one with the Brotherhood of God by opening their minds to the open channel that brings communication between us.* Be of good cheer on this."

It was hard for me to conceive of such a selfless group of spirits as this Brotherhood. Mentally I endowed them with my characteristics—impatience, weariness over repetition, despair and disappointment over other people's actions. Yes, a stubborn doubt persevered about their willingness to do what they claimed—help me fulfill my God-potential. These thoughts of mine, for I never uttered them aloud or typed them on paper, brought a vigorous response from these advanced spirits.

"The Brotherhood of God always has the person's best interests in mind. There is no puny motive on our part to get something for ourselves. There is no grumbling when we are asked to help. No one says, 'There you go again, asking for help.' When you ask, we come. This is our joy, our great wonderful pleasure. No time of night or day matters to us here, for we do not observe time as you observe it. We have no greater motive than to be one with God. We give you this prayer of growth— may God give you His great gifts with our help.

"The Brotherhood is real. We have lived on the earth plane many times. The spiritual law says that we on this plane must live again and again in order to understand the lessons life has to teach us. In one lifetime this is not possible."

(There will be more on God's plan—reincarnation— throughout this book.)

"I know that people have need of us," the message continued. "I hear their cries on this plane. The Brotherhood takes each cry into the mind of the Universal God. The cry may be to no purpose, but it is a cry. We go to that person to try to help. But no help is possible until the person requests our help. The reason for our inability to help some people is that we all have free will. That way when we choose the godly way, our perfection is true, not a facade."

I asked the messenger from the Brotherhood what sort of things people want help with. "They want help to grow into the wonderful people they know they should be. Not 'should' in an outer way, but 'should' in the inner way. The 'should' means that we grow to the extent of our concepts. If we conceive of ourselves as wonderful human beings, then we become wonderful human beings. But if we give ourselves the picture of the poor little creature, the one who is undeserving, the one who is hopeless about life, then we become that person. We want to become the person we 'should' be—the one we conceive of."

"Can you help me to develop a better picture of myself?" I asked.

"Yes. We build into your mind impressions of your best qualities. We build the concept into a beautiful creature so that you can indeed become that which you visualize. The mind is the key here. The mind is the truth of our beings. The mind gives us entry to the soul."

"But what about brain-damaged people? You can't reach them, I suppose." I received an illuminating reply to this question.

"The truth here is that these people will develop within, for they have no truth of their own disability to impede them. We connect easily with those who open their minds, no matter the condition of the brain. The mind is not the brain. The mind is that which gives you the truth of your being, that which is the eternal part of you, the real. The mind gives you the spark of life, the God-spark, that which we call the soul."

"Then parents who have brain-damaged children should understand that growth of the spirit still continues?" I asked.

"These children who come into this world with brains that do not serve them well may grow even more than those who have a great intellect. The brain is the bodily function, but mind is the spirit function. The spirit is eternal. The body is temporary. That is the truth.

"The Brotherhood reaches out to all. Those who wait until their deathbeds may open their minds to us to help them and we do. No Brother says to the person, 'You have waited too long, old man. You're out of luck.' The person is always helped. We do not see you with the eyes of judgment, but with the eyes of the good that we might do to help you connect with the God of your being.

"There is no circumstance that thought of our help cannot put right. We on this plane—the Brotherhood—team up with you to give the good news to you. Tell your readers that no belief or disbelief hampers our work. One can be without faith in any of the truths he has heard to date, but when he turns to us, we will help him find his own truth. The only truth to trust is that which grows inside you anyway. To reject other truths is merely the expression of your inner being to find your own truth. The growth of the spirit is the main idea. Keep this in mind."

I queried about help from these advanced spirits in the matter of personal safety. "Help may be possible if the person believes in that help instantaneously. The protection may happen, but not always, because people panic when the crisis comes and turn their minds to the overwhelming tragedy."

I asked if the Brotherhood will come when we ask for healing for someone else. "The one asked for is open to us, of course, but your pleading has nothing to do with it. God's help is for all, no matter the circumstances. The truth is that God is the God of the Universe, all-powerful, all-knowing. He opens us to all the good gifts if we open our minds to these gifts. Properly used, the energy of the universe can heal. We can help the ill person. The growing person can help too. Healing is another subject, and it would take a long time to explain the working of it."

What an intriguing answer—one I want to follow up on someday soon. Those advanced souls—the Brotherhood—stand at the ready to teach us and help us grow. Whether we accept any religious theology or not, all of us can relate to the concept of help from those who understand what life is all about.

CHAPTER 2

FORMING A PARTNERSHIP

*What can I expect from a partnership with the
Brotherhood, and what do they expect from me?*

Forming a partnership with the Counselor/Brotherhood of
God is not a complicated business. There is no mysterious or
occult session needed. The prerequisite, as I understand it, is
to make a request. In this way we give permission to those
advanced spirits to enter our minds and give us their counsel.

"Many need to have partners—the more tangible proof of
God," said my communicator. To me in particular, "This tangible proof is in our written communication, of course." And
again to us all, "The proof is also in the open channel between
us and the person who invites our help. We will manifest in
one way or another if a person's mind is turned toward us in
the promise that we make. This is the truth."

You may wonder, as I did, why this group of souls wants to do
this obviously difficult work of communicating with us and
helping us through our problems and onward to our spiritual
growth. Who are they?

They told me that they came into being in the beginning of
God's establishment of the earth. However, they do not think
the truth of how they came into being is important at this
point. "We enter to help. This is our entire thought," they say.
"Why concern yourself with who we were on the earth plane?

The point is who we are now. That is what matters. We entered life even as you have entered life, but our reality is NOW, not the past."

However, they did give some insight into the past, as we on earth figure time. "The Brotherhood began on earth, and it continued on this plane to help others still on the earth plane. But it was hard to get in touch and to maintain contact. Therefore, Jesus went back to earth to be the Godself that entered into flesh and made contact with these helpers. He gave a pattern of prayer, of healing and of direction. He gave fully of himself there, but he made use of the advanced spirits here. He grew in that lifetime into a full potential realized. He did this because he used the help from this plane, not because he was perfect to begin with, not because he was God to start with. Now he wants to open this channel wider than ever to encourage others to use this channel to enrich their lives to the perfection which is easily within their grasp if they use the help that we can give."

I come from a traditional Protestant Christian background, and these words seemed sacrilegious. My thoughts were enough to trigger this answer: "There is no sacrilege when we know God is the source of all energy that is given. God is the source of this wonderful open channel that can tenderly take this concept to your consciousness. People so often feel lonely that there is no friend, no one to care. But in this Brotherhood there is caring. Entities will come to fill you if you seek to be filled."

Later the messenger added to this concept of who and what the Brotherhood is and why it exists. "If you want to help others, if you want to be God's emissary, then this is work that you may want to do here on this plane when you come. Remember, we do not enter the earth plane to become one with you. The truth is that we enter to help you unite with God-mind even as Jesus did." These Counselors insist that each of us must set our own goals in life. Then they will help us go to God-mind to reach these goals.

If a partnership is to be formed between you and the Brotherhood of God, there must be communication. Here we come to the heart of the matter of making the partnership a working, practical one. Half the partnership is ethereal and half is earthly. Apparently these in the next plane can hear us easily enough, but how do we hear them?

First let's consider the process of automatic writing, which is what I use. A well-known writer of psychic books wrote that *anyone* can do automatic writing. Not being particularly psychic myself—certainly no more so than the average person—I knew I did not possess any special powers.

I simply sat down at a table with several sheets of 8 1/2 by 11 inch paper and some well-sharpened pencils. I had nothing in particular in mind—certainly not the Brotherhood of God. Had I sought a teacher or counselor immediately, I could have progressed much faster. The thing was, I didn't know exactly what I wanted. I sat for ten or fifteen minutes with very little happening. My pencil seemed pushed now and then to make sweeps across the page, and that's all. Disappointed, I nevertheless determined to try it for several days at the same hour for 15 to 20 minutes.

By the third or fourth day my pencil was practicing large "o's," large "l's" and some figure "8's" across the page. The "8's" were sideways as if to indicate infinity. Yes, it grew boring, and yes, I wanted to give it up because it seemed so silly. Then I began to get messages—many of them frantic. One that persisted over a period of several days was, "Mother is alive. Mother is alive." (My pencil pushed heavily and quickly across the page. "Mother frees you from her promise. She must be on her way now to the promised land." This message never got delivered, for I have no idea who Mother is or whom she wants to free. But there was no doubt in my mind that some soul needed to impart these words to someone still on the earth plane.

Two letters, written together like initials, began to appear each day. Finally the writer revealed himself as a person I had known well when he lived on this earth. He had problems because he was very attached to someone still on earth, a someone he wanted to make changes that affected his growth. I wasn't sure at this point that I wanted to get this kind of message. I had stepped into someone else's personal life, and I felt uncomfortable.

My early experiences in automatic writing brought me into contact with many spirit entities, including my father. One day my father "took my pencil" and told me what he is doing with his life now. His greatest concern is for my brother and his family even as it was while he lived on earth. He had hated me, he said, during the last few years of his life because he was in a nursing home, and he named the home. I asked him how he felt toward me now. He said he no longer hates me because he isn't in the nursing home now. "Love," he said, "is the most important thing to me now."

It was not until I asked specifically for a teacher—someone who could help me with my life, someone who could filter out the many frantic messages that I could do nothing about, did I meet the Brotherhood of God. An entity called Love signed in each day. Our communication was poor due to my inadequate reception. Love would begin some fascinating statement and then I could not get the ending. Crucial words were not expressed, and there was much frustration on my part. But having gone this far, I stayed with it, however grimly.

I dated each day's writing. And as Love helped me along, I began to type each day's written work no matter how full of omissions. Day by day I could see more and more complete statements, and I grew encouraged. And the writing was not without humor. I like to read mystery stories, and one day in the midst of trying to get the words down on paper, came this statement: "I think the mystery stories you read cloud your mind."

One day I received instructions to go to my typewriter and place my fingers on the keys. Typing made communication much easier. Always, before I wrote or typed the communication, I tried to still my mind, empty it of thought, and then I prayed for protection and guidance.

Love no longer signed in. Someone else from the Brotherhood took over. This entity taught me how to concentrate in a way that would enable the messenger and me to be on the same wave length. I received directions to hold a picture in my mind, a picture of the soft earth, which is my mind, and a plow, which is the Brotherhood. The plow turned the soft and willing earth, and as it did so, I finally began to type with some speed as my fingers reached for the keys. I am not sure even now just how this works. I seem to have impressions of the words just before I type them, but there are some times when I go very slowly awaiting the impulse that moves my fingers.

According to my communicator, not everyone is given the same picture to use in making contact. The picture suits me and reaches my particular understanding. I have never read in any other psychic literature of this method of contact.

Many churches, ministers and religious people warn against doing automatic writing as if it in itself is evil. I made this statement to these Brothers who dismissed the idea of evil with a tongue-in-cheek comment. "On the earth plane there is much fear." I was told that the immediate need here is to be assured that God is real and that the earth life is our temporary home. "You on earth do not live there permanently. You bring your soul there for growth, not permanent habitation."

I asked if someone might give suggestions on automatic writing as a means of contacting them. "This Brotherhood will receive any person who wishes to make an open contact with us. If the person wants to be in communication by investing time on your plane, then the writing may be the best means of communication."

But they do not rule out other means of contact. "If you open your mind, and open your heart, too, then we come to you to help. But if you want on the open channel, you must give time on your plane to get this. It is the payment, so to speak. But the time need not be overly long. It can be only a short concentrated time, a time of going to God the Father in prayer and a time of important growing." By "important growing" the Brother is referring to a person's attention to the open channel that makes communication possible.

I asked how a person can open his mind and heart. "If a person wants to contact the Brotherhood, the sincere desire is enough to make the contact."

"But there is no proof of this contact!" I protested.

"This kind of contact is not visible to you. You must make the point that *you* cannot *see* us, but nevertheless the communication is there. You feel the keys of this typewriter depress beneath your fingers, but others may use a pencil and let their hand become the hand of the Brotherhood. Others may be good listeners, better than you are, and they may hear our voice. There is one other way too. By taking your inner growth tone, the wave length of the energy that courses through you, you may get on this wave length where you may be in the growth pattern that we are. Both the wave lengths must be synchronized with one another. But only those who understand physics may understand this. These helpers go into the world to be there on your plane. But so many do not take heed. There the Brotherhood goes, going to your support and aid, but so few heed them. People do things the hard way—alone."

Another day my communicator had this to say about how people can make use of the open channel. "This is the way: To you who would use the typewriter, this is a good way. To others who do not type or who won't consider this method, there is another way. Our plane and your plane coming together is to be understood. A person may listen to his inner voice. This is fine. It is good, but obviously not many know how to listen to the inner voice. The thrust of this message is that there is a way for all. And it can be as certain as writing letters. We write letters, don't we? We expect answers, right? Then this way is most sure. The inner voice may be mystical to many, you see. And it is subject to the subconscious, but so is the writing." (To me: "You even have trouble with putting your subconscious out of the way, right?)

"This is the way to communicate—to meditate, to listen, to write us and let us answer through your fingers. The Brotherhood does not care which method. Use whatsoever you will, but open your mind to this open channel that you may not waste your earth life. Be assured that this earth life is the temporary life and your next life is the real one. On this plane you have the identity that is permanent. In earth life you have an impermanent identity."

And finally, "Jesus came there to show people how to take their growth seriously and to live according to God's best plan for uniting the two planes. The Brotherhood became the Counselor that Jesus promised. Use it. This group of advanced spirits is not mystical nor is it open to evil. It is incorruptible."

CHAPTER 3

GROWING INTO THE
PERSON YOU WANT TO BE

Why must I live many lifetimes?

"Reincarnation is God's plan for our growth. We need to understand this plan in order to make the most of our opportunity. Be open on this matter. Reincarnation is just a fact of your life and of mine and of others' lives. No immediate doubt will erase this fact. Just like the earth is round—doubt will not change it."

Most of us have been taught that this one lifetime is IT. There is no more. The idea of living lifetime after lifetime in order to grow spiritually presents a challenge to many of us. Questions leap to mind. If reincarnation is true, who was I in a previous lifetime? Where did I live? Those in the Brotherhood insist that the only important question is, What did I learn?

"You create the person you want to be by the growth you make in your earth lives. You choose the person you want to be."

References to reincarnation appeared again and again in my writing. I asked why we need a belief in reincarnation.

"This belief is needed just as a belief in God is needed. The plan of lifetime after lifetime helps us to gain a new perspective of ourselves and our progress. The lifetime you lived earlier enters into this lifetime as lessons learned. This truth from previous lifetimes opens us to greater and greater use of

God-energy. Truth goes into our beings and it stays there. Then the next lifetime is the one in which you can use the truth you have learned before. Then you progress to another goal, and so it goes on and on."

Since reincarnation affords us many opportunities to grow into the person we want to be, I asked if someone keeps a record of our progress. "No! The one who keeps count is you. You evaluate your own progress. That is why we enter into earth lives so often. We do not get the wide picture of our good except by lifetime after lifetime."

Soul growth—not an easy concept for me to understand. My communicator knew my mind-struggle on the subject. "The growth of the soul is the part that you must get straight. Growth is of God. Growth is God. Growth is happiness, satisfaction, the best that you can conceive and even better. You cannot imagine this perfect growth, for you still strive toward it. But soul growth is not misery, not hardship. Growth is goodness and brotherhood and honor on earth and in heaven."

Though growth is not easy to accomplish, these advanced spirits urge us to keep the faith that God is in charge and we will be one with Him. Furthermore, they promise to keep us on track in our thinking and in our open minds. "The Brotherhood of God, which is Christ, is your way to become the person you want to be."

" 'Choose today whom ye will serve ... as for me and my house, we will serve the Lord.' (Joshua 24:15) I know you remember this. The Bible is full of these admonitions to keep the faith. Not always did the writers understand why, but they knew it was important."

My traditional religious background was difficult to put aside in order to open my mind to truth. When anyone in the Brotherhood reminded me of those Biblical admonitions, right away I reverted to old ways of thinking. Therefore, I asked, "So many of us want to 'succeed.' By this we mean financially with symbols of success—like lovely possessions, social recognition, and even power. Doesn't this goal work against a goal of soul growth?"

"I only know," came the answer, "that no matter what road you take, growth is possible in the earth life when people turn to God in the matter of learning their lessons thoroughly and becoming open to the Brotherhood of God.

"This is the law: No matter your riches, the growth of spirit is possible when you turn to this open channel to receive your guidance. Then you are open to spirit, open to the Brotherhood, open to God's plan."

In the New Testament, among the many stories of Jesus, is one that has always given me pause for thought. It is the story of a rich ruler who asked Jesus what he should do to have eternal life. Jesus asked him if he had kept the commandments, and the ruler said he had. Then Jesus asked him to sell all that he had and to distribute it to the poor, but the ruler went away sorrowfully, for he was very rich. (Luke: 18:18-23) Then came Jesus' remark that is quoted again and again. "How hard it is for those who have riches to enter the kingdom of God." (Luke: 18:24) Others who heard this exchange wondered aloud how anyone could hope for eternal life, but Jesus assured them that with God all things are possible.

I asked about this story. "It means that the rich ruler did not open his mind to counsel, nor did he open his mind to the Brotherhood of God. He wanted to direct things himself, to be the author of the plan and not let God author the plan. We do not grow until we let God author the plan."

I reminded my correspondent that the ruler had kept all the commandments. "That is so. He gave the law his attention. People do this today. They give the law their attention, both temporal and church law. This is the point of this whole interchange. God wants the ruler to put Him first, to grow, to become one with the God-self. This God-self has the pure thought of God in it. To put God first is to give no thought to the church's wonderful rules. These rules do not give growth. They give stagnation. The churches hold the church laws intact, but they do not free the individual to put God first. The law tells him how to behave. Jesus told the ruler to sell what he had to get the ruler's attention, to get him off the center point of the law. The law gave the ruler his assurance. He went away unable to get his center changed."

The person I want to be—who is she? Yes, WHO AM I? This is the eternal question we strive to answer. Books, pamphlets, articles and poems use this theme of "Who am I?" over and over again. In our most secret places, we paint a picture of ourselves, a picture that answers that question, a picture of the person we want to be. Those in the Brotherhood call this picture "God's plan within you." And they tell me that when we stray from that which is creating the person we want to be, we become dissatisfied with our lives and feel within us that we are going amiss. "This is the point of reincarnation—that you have the chance to go forth in the midst of temptation and enact your mission. The choice of your various lives is part of your growth. You go with some purpose in mind. The life experience is your chance to enact that purpose."

The thought must come that if we return again and again, why isn't this world by now filled with good and great souls? Why is there still greed, inhuman cruelty, hatred? "This is the reason," came the answer. "Today people on your plane come from this plane in great numbers, and on this plane we do not always grow enough to be advanced souls on the earth plane. But many do come that are advanced. They try to lead the world into peace and growth in common concerns. But there is a need of more advanced souls. The word on this is that people return to accomplish growth, but some do not understand this goal. They return just to return. They do not develop there or here."

"Who we were before," I asked, "apparently does not matter so much as what we were, right?"

The answer came quickly. "This is right. Who you are is the puzzle that you put together in your lives. You are making that person in your lives. You want your personal spirit to become more Godlike. You want to work in the enlightenment of Spirit, to live in that Spirit, to energize your soul to be more Godlike. Jesus spoke of this."

"If I could ask Jesus right now what is the greatest commandment, would he still say, 'You shall love the Lord your God with all your heart, and with all your soul, and with all your mind'? And would he still say, 'A second is like it, you shall love your neighbor as yourself'?" (Matthew 22:37-39)

"This is what Jesus says: That love is the greatest manifestation of God. Growth in spirit is evidenced by the love you bear for one another."

"Is this like doing good deeds?" I asked.

"Good deeds are part of it, of course. But love is greater than good deeds. Love opens your heart to one another. Love makes your growth complete. Love brings you close to God. Be open to God in love and He will guide you in good deeds that need doing. You cannot make love happen by doing good deeds. You cannot make God come into your heart. You cannot force the spiritual growth. You get only hard knocks in your trying. You get a briny taste because you put salt into the work instead of love. This is the open channel's truth. This is Jesus' truth."

I commented that the idea of "Let go and let God" must be a good truth to keep in mind.

"That is right," came the response. "The open channel's work is to let God work through you. You need to focus on the open channel to get your emptying in eventual control. Empty yourself before you fill to become your best self." I asked if "emptying" is the same as "meditation" and the Brotherhood agreed that they are the same. "Empty yourself," the words continued, "and then let God work in you."

Love, as my communicator describes it and as Jesus describes it, has not been easy to practice. I explained that I find it hard to love some people in this open, really selfless way. I expected an unsympathetic answer, but this is what I received. "This is the way to handle this: Be open to others in their needs. Be open to them in their growth. Be open to them in their search for truth. But open yourself only on these matters—not personal matters. Do empty yourself of anger and bitterness. These block the open channel, keeping the Brotherhood from going to you to give you help."

Later writing clarifies further what is meant by demonstrating and manifesting love for one another. "This kind of love is the agape love—the love that helps one another, not a love that encompasses their being with affection. This agape love is one of caring that unites us into brothers. It is not the love between man and woman or parent to child. It is the love that God presents us with in this world—the entering of His loving warm spirit into your spirit. That is the truth. The only reason you go to us is to be open to receive gifts such as 'love' from God."

I looked up "agape" in my dictionary. The definition reads, "divine love, God's love for man."

Tragedies within our community, even our own family, hurt us and present many "why" type questions. Why did this innocent person have to die? Why did this young person commit suicide? I mentioned my grief over a tragedy in our small community to my counselor. "These events open us to truth. These open us to seek the answers that God has. You open yourselves to this seeking immediately, and the problems will be answered and met. But if you persist with the questions, the problem stays and stays and stays."

The advanced spirits in the Brotherhood of God insist that growth of our souls is the answer to life's questions. The more we grow, the wider our view. The wider our view, the less we agonize over life's injustice. We see the part instead of the whole.

"If a person does not give credence to Jesus Christ or the Christian religion," I asked my source, "would he find you believable?"

Here is the answer: "It depends on that person's wonderful growth in spirit. People grow in spirit in various ways, not just Christian methods. Not just Moslem or any other religion. They grow because this is their intention when they come to this life. They may forget about God, but in their growth breathes that spirit which is God. They may call it humanism or they may call it personality, but whatever they call it, that spirit is of God."

Growing into the person you want to be may be an attractive goal, but the accomplishment of it definitely takes time and thought. My source puts it this way: "Be open on the subject of the good power that is available to you from this plane. The power is here and it is open to you. Enter into the wonderful Brotherhood of God that has so much to give you. Open your mind to the wonder, to the great open channel that feeds you all this power on growth."

CHAPTER 4

CONSIDERING THE GOD OF THE UNIVERSE

Why isn't my present concept of God good enough?

When I was a child and said the word "God," I visualized a large man with white hair and beard, a man with kind eyes, a man with arms that reached out to embrace me. As I matured that picture faded, but it never completely went away.

One sub-zero day in February, ice and snow keeping me homebound, a messenger from the Brotherhood began to instruct me about God. Thereupon my childish image of a saintly old man was blown away like dust. "Nobody knows the God that is at the center of the universe. He is the God that brings us order. He is the God that brings us knowledge. But He is not known. The God that loves you is known. They are one and the same, yes. But there is a matter of understanding. We must be able to understand this God of order and knowledge to know Him. God is much more than even Jesus explained to us, for Jesus was sent for one purpose only—to show people God's gifts of love and guidance, His mercy and the Brotherhood of Believers. Jesus was not sent to discuss and teach on the universe. People were not ready for the message of the universal God. They were only ready for the message of their one God as they understood Him."

I asked if we are ready now—in this latter part of the 20th century—to understand the universal God, and this is the response: "This is the time, for God is the planner and the operator of the universal organization. Grow in your understanding of these two planes working together, and you will enter into the understanding of God as the God of the Universe.

"To understand the meaning of God of the Universe, people must widen their concepts of God. The God that loves them is one concept. The God of power is another concept. The truth that comes with trying to understand this more advanced concept is worth going after.

"This concept of the God of power is what people want in their lives. The power is to be used for God's good purpose—not on the personal level. To manifest the pure energy of God one must know the purpose—to give good gifts to reinforce the worth of our beings, to reinforce our growth, to reinforce the pure intelligent truth of the God-self.

"To use the power of God in this way is to use it rightly. The power will never run out; it will never give way to emptiness. But the principle must always be applied. This power is the greatest source to create the outer things that our bodies need to live in peace, as well as to create the inner things that we need to grow to our full potential. This power comes from God who is Principle Himself. There is that aspect of God—the power principle or the God of the Universe. This God has many concepts to give us, many things to present to our minds. Those who open their minds to this God-concept of the universal presence will get into the truth of the God-self faster than the ones who deny God as the universal presence."

Understanding the God of the Universe is not easy. Nevertheless, those in the Brotherhood believe it important for people on this plane to open their minds to the ultimate growth—oneness with the God of the Universe. Here is another discourse on the subject: "God is at the center of this universe. God is the power, the glue that holds it all together. God is the good that men do. God is the good that you do. But He is also the One whose words come through this open channel, the God who belongs to all, He who becomes your mentor. God is all that is good, pure, and great. He has His helpers in the best of these advanced spirits. We try to be one with Him in our work here. We become His in spirit and power so that we can carry His work to your plane. God is power. God is good. God is spirit. God is real. Reality is spirit.

"Be one with God in your heart. The Father, God, is one with you. You, like Jesus, are called to be the Christ on your plane. You are the Christ in action. Think on this." My correspondent then spoke for the Brotherhood itself. "God is our Father too. He holds our good in His thought. He holds our purity in His heart. We belong to Him because we on this plane find Him irresistible. We want to belong to this good power because we find in it great joy and great growth."

Trying to compare this concept to something else I already understand, I compared God, Jesus and the Brotherhood to a corporate structure which I called a "hierarchy of heaven." Here is the response: "This hierarchy is not right. The idea of a corporate organization will not do at all. The God of the Universe is not the head of a company. We are not workers in a growth machine. We on this plane do not work on the idea of profit. Be clear on this. We on this plane open ourselves to God, growing into His good persons, not his good people who get material rewards on their work. Growth is not profit here. Growth is the spirit of God, of Good, of Perfection, bringing us more good in our lives than we can ever visualize."

The reply came with vigorous and rapid energy. I had taken a wrong turn in my thinking; quickly this Brother straightened out my misconceptions.

Like a good teacher, my correspondent kept at the task of teaching me what God is. "We in the Brotherhood understand that God is the supreme spiritual law. He is the One who introduces us to the good that we try to do. Jesus works with us as the open channel through which we see God Himself."

My concept of God will continue to change as will yours if you go to the advanced spirits for counsel, for this is their promise: "The Brotherhood is helping you to accept the concept of God that we seek to teach you. Understand that God is much that we cannot explain to you because you do not place your being in His hands wholly. You hold back a part of yourself, yes? You go to God often, but you hold back on many things. This holding back keeps you from understanding God in the way you ask to understand."

I asked about prayer to God through Jesus and through saints. "These people need pictures to help them visualize God. They do, in fact, open their minds to the idea that God IS, but they seldom go far in their spiritual growth because they believe in a limited concept of God that in turn limits them. Believe in the omnipresent and omnipotent God and open your mind to this plane to help you grow. The Brotherhood of God will be there for you. We have no statue, no picture, no tangible presence on the earth plane, but we in this plane open ourselves to God through Jesus Christ and can help you do the same."

On another day, my source further enlarged my understanding of God. "Give yourself to God wholly by telling Him that you do this. Telling Him has the effect of putting you into our hands to hold you to the promise you made to be one with Him. Make God your center and He will keep you on the track. That way you become whole. You become the walking persona of God's peace."

"Instead of asking for things," I inquired, "should I put my energy into letting go of my own ego and trust God to give me what is good?"

"That is on the mark!"

I asked if the evangelists are right, that we must let go completely of our own selfish desires and let God take over. The response was as follows: "That message is all right up to the point of what you believe about God. If God is the reflection of your own thoughts, then you are giving yourself to a limited concept of God. But if you give yourself totally to God, whoever He is, and depend on the Brotherhood to help you, then you'll progress beyond the limiting thoughts you hold of God."

I have been taught that the Bible is divinely inspired. However, I find parts that seem inconsistent with the view of God as all GOOD. I told my teacher/counselor that I cannot worship a God that is all GOOD but who at the same time is sending pestilence, famine or other ills upon people as a punishment for their sins.

"This part of the Bible that you find inconsistent is the written word of the people, not of God. People go into life believing that God must be on their level of being. Therefore God is good in the same way they on earth are good, and He is given to temper outbursts as they are given to temper outbursts. They wrote of a God they could understand in line with what they wanted Him to be. This is why you read of a God who punishes in such terrible ways. In those days pestilence was real. It had to be explained. But they did not have the enlightenment to understand God.

"Nor do people today understand God. They blame Him for the terrible things that happen to them. They do not see that they use God to explain their feelings and the happenings in life. God neither brings sickness nor gives us anything else that brings us misery. He is all GOOD. But there on your plane there is the fact of disease and the fact of evil. The people blame these negative things on God in order to explain them to themselves. Deep down they know that God is their reality, but they have lost the meaning of God."

"Is the Bible my best guide for living?" I asked.

"This Bible is a guide for living. It is divinely inspired. Those who wrote it believed wholeheartedly in God as the ultimate reality. But your own life is not the point of the Bible. The Bible gives you the progression of thought about God. There is no way to present it except by way of people's lives. Therefore, you read of Noah and Moses and others as they opened themselves to God's direction in their lives. They were great people, but they are not you."

I asked what is the best way I can use the Bible to enrich my own life, and my teacher said I am to read it with the understanding that they have given me. I asked for comment on the New Testament. "These stories show you again the gigantic leap forward people took when Jesus' message came. It shows too that while there were great leaps forward, there was reluctance to let go of old concepts. That is why the people had to find Jesus the God, the only Son of God. They could not conceive of themselves being the perfection that Jesus is. They could not look at the window (Jesus) and see God beyond. They painted the window in their own colors so they could not see through it. And they said, "Lo, yonder window is really God."

The Brotherhood's communicator makes it clear that

though the Bible is inspirational, I must find my own path to oneness with God. I asked them to discuss this thought. "God has a path for you indeed. But this path is not the only possible path. You have choices. God is flexible. He has this wonderful choice for you, and you become your own guide. But you need help along the way due to life's problems and your needs. We are that help, that opening that leads you to God. We are here to be your counselor, your help, your strength when needed. Be open to this Brotherhood and we will be open to you. But we cannot act unless there is an awareness within you that we on this plane have help for you. This awareness is the key to unlocking the partition between us."

The awareness that those in the Brotherhood speak of is the not-so-secret way of opening ourselves to all that the God of the Universe has to offer. "If you think of good that you need, like love or understanding, or getting great power, then these will go to you by transfer to you from us. These gifts of God are stored here to take as you need them. The principle or law of God is that you receive that which you can bring to your mind. The God of power, the God of the Universe—these concepts produce these gifts in your life."

CHAPTER 5

WALKING INTO THE BRIGHT SUN OF GOD

How can counseling help me to grow in spiritual
understanding?

"It is now important to be prepared to walk into the bright sun of God," wrote my teacher from the next plane of life. I took my fingers from the typewriter keys and reread the message. What a beautiful metaphor and how much to the point of my conversations with the Brotherhood of God.

When I began an experiment in automatic writing, the writing that comes through me but not from me, I had no idea what would happen, if anything. However, after reading books in the psychic field by several reputable authors, I knew I had to try this activity myself. In Chapter 2, I explained the details of how I began and what happened in this experiment.

Meeting the Counselor, the one promised by Jesus, in such a concrete way changed my life irrevocably. The Jesus I knew before I met the Counselor/Brotherhood was mystical and perfect beyond imitation. The Jesus I used to know came to this earth plane with powers that ordinary people cannot be expected to have. The Jesus I know now is a practical advanced soul who became on earth what we're all expected to be one day—one with God.

I see Jesus now as the one who threw back the doors to heaven, so to speak, so we can accomplish our goals here on this earth plane. He invited us to make use of the promised Counselor, the Brotherhood of God, who acts as an open channel between us and God and between God and us. The communication goes both ways.

I wrote this chapter once and when I finished, I asked someone from the Brotherhood to comment on it. "I think you need to have more on the wonderful goodness of God. Growth is the good truth. Growth is the God-plan that God wants emphasized. Take more time on this. The Brotherhood gives people help in the godly way of life. In your own story you get away from this help. Be into this work now."

I reread the chapter. The critical commentary was right. Carried away with journalistic fervor, I wrote pages on my conversations with my communicator. I formed a personality of the teacher. But I missed the entire point of the chapter—to explain how the Brotherhood of God, who acts as the Counselor, is helping me to grow spiritually.

When this body took its first breath, the soul that entered it had already lived many lifetimes. Reincarnation makes sense to me because I now see the divine plan in it. When I meet a child who has brain damage or a physical disability or who is abandoned or abused, I know this one lifetime is not all that child will have. What the child learns from his experience, however, is the point. It is the point of my life, too. Reincarnation assures that all our development, all our happiness and joy is not dependent on this one lifetime. We come again and again until we grow into mature souls that need never come this way again to learn life's lessons.

My communicator puts it this way: "God plans this good method (reincarnation) that souls may try again and again to grow into that which they are intended to become—their full potential. To understand reincarnation, one needs to give the growth idea the consideration it deserves. Growth is the purpose of life. Only growth. Growth is the spirit that comes into relationship with God who empties that soul of all ego and fills it with the God-life. Reincarnation is the way; growth is the purpose. Reincarnation takes the soul the long way to attain truth, but it is the plan that works. Growth comes with lifetime after lifetime.

"The time between lives is spent here on this plane where each soul contemplates his last lifetime and plans what he must do to continue growth. Then as the soul goes out again, there is a plan to carry out. That's the way it works.

"Those who do not grow, they go on lifetime after lifetime, the ones who know not who they are or why they come to earth in the first place. Many of them give up in life, become the total grumblers or the total criminals, or the suicides. They intend to accomplish nothing in life because they came without a plan. They wander in the earth plane lost in their own emptiness."

The teacher assures me that my true home is in the next plane, that I have family there who care about me. Though I do not remember anything about such a life, I am assured again and again that when I leave this earth plane (die), that I will be joyous in my reunion with those who await me there. This lifetime is temporary; my true life is on the next plane. I believe this about myself, for my life makes more sense in this perspective than it did when I believed that my earthly relationships were all I had in the way of loving family and true friends.

Not only does reincarnation give me a better perspective of my own life, it helps me to accept the tragedies of life with a belief in divine justice and divine good. When a person dies in an accident, by murder or by his own hand, I know that the soul still lives. I know that soul is welcomed home by those whose love is eternal. I know God's plan will let that soul try life again. The same is true of those I love—friends and family. When they die I grieve, oh yes! But grief passes and acceptance of God's plan takes its place.

I received a gift from the Brotherhood one day. "Today is the only one of this kind. You may question the ones who have gone before. Today you may go to them. Today you may be the questioner." I was delighted but unprepared. Later I wished my list of names had been longer.

I asked first about a man from my community who lived a full life and died when he was in his seventies. "He is the best one whom we have on the matter of growth. He chose one plan to demonstrate in his last life, and he has done it. He is the one who goes forth from here to help others, and he helps his wife with his presence (on the earth plane). It is the truth of his growth that he was born to be open to others on both planes." I asked if this man chose to be black in his recent lifetime. "This is true. He chose this. He is now the open channel to many black people there. On this plane there is no black or white or Chinese or other differences. We are spirit here."

I asked about a young man who died some years ago when he was only twenty years old. I learned that though he died young, he had accomplished much growth of his spirit during his lifetime. "He is not the same person you knew on the earth plane. He is now more mature."

Of course I asked about members of our family. Imagine my surprise to learn that my father-in-law re-entered earth life ten years ago. My mother-in-law, I was told, is very busy helping other people, helping them to be aware of the Brotherhood's help. She is with our daughter, who is in Italy, helping her granddaughter to grow and accomplishing her own growth, too.

I asked about a man my husband and I knew for many years, a man who worked in Washington, D.C. "This is very interesting. Don (fictitious name) has much to offer. He is the open channel on the government here. He energizes the open channel so that those officials go to this channel instead of entering only into their own understanding. I told you this was interesting. He is an excellent illustration of how to use growth to become the person he wants to be—helpful to his fellows. This is the word: He is the open channel on the government. He cares about his wife, Ann (fictitious name). Her interests are his concern, and he is with her daily to help her turn to the open channel."

The open channel, remember, is the Christ within us all. The Brotherhood explained how this works. "Don is the open channel by letting his Christ self merge with the Christ self of others. Then the channel forms."

Yes, growth of the spirit is what life—here and on the next plane—is all about. When we get this part straight in our minds, these advanced spirits tell me, our lives fall into the pattern that leads us to our own full potential—our oneness with God.

I hope it does not seem frivolous to mention my concern over our dog friends. My husband and I have always had one or two dogs in our home. I asked if there is a survival of that energy that was our dog. "This is the law on animals. They put the growth of their spirits into the hands of God. They open their eyes to good or they open their eyes to bad. Then they must become new creatures that work out their development, even as people do. But they will always be animals. They are not people, but they have the gift of God's creative spirit in them."

God's plan for growth is perfect. Life does indeed give us many challenges to help us grow, and none greater than the conflicts between people. One relationship in my life has defied my fervent efforts to make it all that is good between people. I asked for insight into this situation. "This other person and you become the golden truth of the law that people cannot become close unless they put the relationship in God's hands. God only can make it good. You wanted to do it all yourself, to put the relationship together, to make it good. The law is that God only can do this."

At first I could not accept this assertion that I tried to make this relationship good all on my own. Hadn't I prayed about it? Hadn't I tried to do my Christian duty to this other person? But truth has a way of opening our inner eyes. I had indeed enacted the role of the noble and self-sacrificing person in the relationship. Why had I tied myself so close to this person when we do not get along well? I didn't wait for guidance from God. I trudged ahead doing what society, my church and my ego dictated.

I am learning to stop pushing in the matter of my relationships—family and friends, too. I will let my plan for living unfold knowing that my one purpose here is growth which is all that I ever hoped to become and even more. My life falls into place—love, prosperity, satisfaction—when I rely on God's plan and the Counselor/Brotherhood's help.

Along this same line, I was cautioned about getting involved in other people's personal heartaches. "You are responsible for yourself," my teacher/counselor told me again and again. "Be a good friend, but do not get personally involved with their problems. Help them turn to the Brotherhood for help." I asked about an elderly friend who has cancer. "This is not your problem," I was told. "This is her time of passing and there is much love surrounding her. Go to her with a cheerful demeanor." Concerned about another friend, I asked how her health was. "This is not your business. This is hers. Be not concerned with the personal. Be there as a friend through all things, but do not let her concerns be yours."

Another time I asked about prayer for others—especially those who are ill. I was told that first I had to be open to the God-force that heals me; then I can include others in that healing force. "Healing others is the work of advanced souls. The best idea is to call upon us to work with the person who is ill."

And this brings me to the scope of our prayers for others. I learned in the churches I attended that prayer for others was my duty and my responsibility. Sometimes people were helped, and sometimes people were not helped. I was to believe that God answered my prayer with a "yes" or with a "no," but He always answered. I gave lip service to this explanation for many years, but never did it satisfy me. Jesus healed anyone who asked him to do so. He always succeeded if the person seeking help believed healing was possible. I asked my friends in the Brotherhood for more explanation.

"This healing by Jesus has no parallel in the earth plane today. Jesus was an advanced soul; that is right. He tried to teach his disciples to do this same healing, and they wondered why they could not always succeed as Jesus did. They thought one only asked God to heal and that was the only thing to do, but there is more, indeed. The truth is that Jesus gave out the God-force that entered his own body. The God-force that Jesus had came to him because he could think it, create it, become it. But though the disciples wondered how it came about, they did not get the thought, the energy to express in them to the extent that Jesus did. Yet they enacted the wonder again and again even as people do today. God-force can become a reality within you, too, *if* a thought is understood to be a thing. But if you cannot think with that degree of truth, then you cannot heal or overcome any obstacle on the earth plane.

"This truth on healing begins with you. Heal yourself first. Then heal the other person. Be one with God yourself; then help the other person become one with God. This is the law on growth."

Now I can understand why I've been disappointed so often in my prayers for others. Putting my relationship with God first in my life is not a selfish act. It is a necessary act to grow into the God-person who can help others. "The purpose of prayer on your plane," my source says, "is to bring you into this one-to-one relationship with God. The purpose of emptying yourself is so God can fill you. Trust in God's plan on this. Prayer on your plane is not one of bringing others to God."

Still and all, I cannot let my concerns about others go by without some attention on my part. My deep-down feeling is that I should storm the gates of heaven on behalf of those I love. I have this passionate desire to help them through their problems, to heal them, to bring them success and happiness. What do I do with this heartfelt desire to make things right in their lives?

Fortunately, there is a way. I had an earnest concern for a friend's daughter. My friend was in mental torment. "The Brotherhood will respond to any concern you express. You want help with Anita (fictitious name), we will go there to help her. Her growth pattern will take time to work, but we will be there with her. That is how it works." Another concern was my friend who seemed close to death. "The truth on her is that she is passing over today. The open channel is there working with her now. This is her time; her growth on the earth plane is over." What more could I ask for than for the Brotherhood of God, nurtured and inspired by Jesus Christ, to be with those for whom I am concerned?

"Reincarnation is the way; growth is the purpose." These words ring through my mind again and again. "You are not just Jean Foster, for you have lived many lifetimes." Since those in the Brotherhood state that people need a clear understanding of reincarnation, I asked for some information on my past lives. My past lives, as told me by my counselor, are interesting, but they are also somewhat disheartening. Only when I keep the matter of growth in mind, can I even accept them.

"This open channel will give you a brief synopsis of this," I was told. "The past lives you have lived all point toward the need to put your ego aside to be the open channel you need to be to let God enter your growth. The God-self that you programmed in advance is the one you try to work out. This lifetime truth has penetrated into your human self to give you the plan of emptying yourself of ego."

I asked for some specific facts of my past lives. "In one lifetime you thought you had the power to judge others. This was your ego. In another you judged the work of your own husband and emptied his good into a prison cell. The next life you put your growth on the matter of helping others give themselves to God, but still you held to dogmatic beliefs. You were not kind. You were not gentle." These facts sum up the few lifetimes the Brotherhood told me about. My sense of privacy cannot permit me to reveal other aspects of my lives. And after reading these illuminating but far from flattering life stories, I have not asked for more. I am glad that the God of the Universe has this plan that has allowed me to try again and again.

Must I return again? This question remains to be answered, of course. Even some advanced souls re-enter life because they want to be here to help others advance in their understanding of the purpose of life. I asked if the people we honor on earth, like Eleanor Roosevelt, Abraham Lincoln, Martin Luther King, Thomas Jefferson, are also honored on the next plane. Here is the answer: "Each of these you mention there on your paper have been the re-entries that will help people during the upcoming turmoil. These souls will be the ones that will give stability to chaotic times. They and many more. Eleanor Roosevelt has returned. This time she picked the black race to be born into. This time she will not be political, but she will be spiritual. This is her plan. The others you mention will give their talents to the widening truth of the open channel. They will help point the way to the Brotherhood who is here for all. They will work to show this truth in wonderful ways. They have their new lives in good order now, and they know how to use thought to manifest good.

"The great souls of this plane often return to the earth plane to help others. They empty themselves of ego to let God fill them. The hope of mankind is in the work of these advanced ones who come now to the earth plane in inconceivable numbers." The messenger added a word of prophecy, both puzzling and reassuring. "Tell others that there will be even more of these advanced souls returning to life. This is the hope for your plane as it enters the new age, the new condition which earth will have."

No matter what changes will come in the "new age," my responsibility is for myself. I want to get my ego out of the way to enable the Brotherhood to put me on the path that leads into the "bright sun of God."

CHAPTER 6

FINDING THE WAY TO TRUTH

Why can't I depend on the Bible and the church to give me truth?

"Truth is that which unites us with God. Truth must be inside ourselves; it is not external. Truth must be of God, or it is not truth. Jesus brings the good news that truth is a living truth, and the way to truth is through the Brotherhood of God, the Counselor that Jesus promised us."

Most of my life I searched for truth in inspirational books, the inspired Word of God—the Bible—and in churches. Surely, I said to my friend from the Brotherhood, there is some church which has the truth. "There is truth in all churches," came the answer. "But no church has it all. Only the individual can open his mind to truth. Your truth is not exactly the same as the truth of another. Be open to all truths. Be true to your own. This is the secret of power. The churches hold worshipers together, but they often limit their understanding. People need to seek their own truth as individuals. This is the real truth."

And what of the Bible? Those in the Brotherhood call the Bible "one source of truth." I asked for commentary about parts of the scripture that puzzled me in some way. Never have I had a more enlightening and inspiring Bible teacher.

In the book of John (20:30), Revised Standard Version, I read, "Now Jesus did many other signs in the presence of the disciples, which are not written in this book; but these are written that you may believe that Jesus is the Christ, the Son of God, and that believing you may have life in his name."

I asked my source what all this means. "John wrote these miracles he saw because they convinced him that Jesus was of God. Therefore, he thought the miracles might convince others too."

I asked if John meant that Jesus was the son of God in the sense that God gave his seed to Mary's womb. "This is the way he believed. But God entered Jesus AFTER he was born. Into Jesus He put His own spirit which gave Jesus his power. Be into the understanding that John opened his eyes to the tradition more than the truth. He took the traditional expectation of the Messiah and put it into the story of Jesus. Therefore, he believed that Jesus was the son of God in a literal sense."

Then my communicator added, "This is the truth that you seek, and this Brotherhood is here to help you find it. Jesus is our brother. Jesus is our open channel to God because he can open himself completely to God and yet be open to us. It is hard to accomplish this, but Jesus did this on earth. He opened himself there to God and to men and women. He opened the eyes of those who could see, and he opened the understanding of those who could understand."

"In general," I asked, "is the Bible account of Jesus correct—his life, his ministry, his death and resurrection, followed by his ascension?"

Here is the answer. "That story is the one that you can understand. But there is far more, of course. Jesus did much more than what is recorded in the Bible. He lived a full life on earth. His ministry is the Bible's concern. But Jesus developed into the soul he was during his ministry through much meditation, prayer, life's lessons learned. Jesus knew he had a purpose that God had sent him for. But he grew into this understanding slowly. He was a child, a boy, a young man who wanted what all young men want—the good things of life. But his purpose kept bringing his attention to God and away from earthly goals. He entered into the Brotherhood of God when he was yet a very young man. He turned his face toward God alone, and he entered his life then as the Son of God."

Many people besides myself are "put off" by the words attributed to Jesus when he supposedly said that it's better to pluck out your eye than to lust or cut off your hand if it does something offensive. A Bible scholar told me that such words are typical of the Middle Eastern exaggeration that is used to get the listener's attention.

My teacher said it is true that these words are indeed exaggeration, that "Jesus never wanted people cutting off an arm or removing an eye in actual practice. He was trying to get people's attention on the matter of their thoughts being the substance of which they build their personalities. If they lust, they build an awareness of the women or men that they desire, and this awareness builds unhappiness over what they have. If they envy others and entertain such thoughts, then they build an awareness of unhappiness over their own circumstances. The exaggerated language was merely a way to get attention fastened on what he was telling them about their minds in action and how their thoughts affect their lives."

"Who is the devil who tempted Jesus?" I asked.

"The devil is that within each of us which invites us to partake of all that life can offer in the way of material gain. If we heed that voice, we turn away from spiritual energy, and we open ourselves to the ultimate unhappiness of a life wasted because it does not develop growth."

"Then Satan is not a fallen angel?" I asked.

"Wonderful that you put these two together, but they are not the same—Satan and the devil. Satan is the Old Testament personality that gives the personification of evil in many fictional stories. But Satan was not an entity that tempted people. He was the one who kept people on the track, so to speak. He gave them pause for thought. He only put to them the questions that they needed to find answers for.

"Now the devil is quite another matter. He is the representation of that within people that brings them to think and talk of the base and ungodly things in life. The devil brings into focus the being which hides within us and is not of God. No devil makes us act. But the devil of baseness and inverted beliefs in God tries to be our mentor in matters of the living of our lives.

"If we give that devil attention, he will build into our lives such a large opening for the bad qualities that we will interact in this life on a low level, a level of cruelty and evil. The result is that we will have wasted a lifetime, and we will later have to overcome it on the next plane—a very difficult thing to do."

Questions flooded my mind. I typed question after question and those from the Brotherhood explained and illuminated all that I asked for. After days of powerful Bible study, I decided that this business of life is meant to be a straightforward matter of working with God in our individual ways. It isn't meant to be complicated.

This advanced spirit agreed. "No, life is not meant to be complicated. Jesus showed us the way. He is the pattern. Open your minds and hearts to the Brotherhood of God, and they will help you understand your purpose. There is help for you. There is no handicap that cannot be overcome, nor any problem that cannot be solved.

"The eternal plan of life is to live again and again until we grow sufficiently never to return to earth. That is the goal of all souls. Never to have to return. This is truth. This is from the Brotherhood of God." The last sentence is the frequent closing these teachers use—the signature that attests that what has been said was of this group of advanced spirits, and I can count on their integrity.

I have often identified myself with Thomas, the disciple who doubted that Jesus had left the tomb. When he actually saw Jesus, Thomas ran to him saying, "My lord and my God!" I asked if the Bible is saying here that Jesus and God are ONE. "Thomas was not speaking for anyone but himself," came the answer. "He said that when he saw Jesus, he believed because he saw the nail holes in Jesus' hands and his pierced side. But Thomas never did understand that Jesus came to reveal the nature of God, not to be God. Thomas was too Jewish to give up the idea of the Messiah that he hoped would come to free Jews and to be their leader on earth."

The Bible says, in the book of John (20:23), that Jesus told his disciples "If you forgive the sins of any, they are forgiven; if you retain the sins of any, they are retained." I told my friend from the Brotherhood that I did not understand these words, nor did I understand why Jesus would give unique power to his disciples. My fingers leaped rapidly from key to key as the answer came.

"Many people want to be forgiven their sins. But they do not give them up to forgiveness. They retain them. They hold them in mind. This scripture says that sins which you forgive will be forgiven. But those you do not forgive, these you will retain. Jesus never gave unique powers to anyone. His truth was for all. The power to forgive is within all. The power to retain is within all."

Sensing a lack of clarity in my thinking, the explanation continued. "It probably is not clear. The power to forgive works two ways: from you to you and from you to others. Be open to forgiveness of your own sins, and be open to forgiveness to the sins of others. This is the truth of Jesus' words here."

Finally after many Bible explanations, my communicator said, "Protestant people give their attention to the Bible to the exclusion of other sources. But the Bible is just one source of truth. If you must go through the Bible step by step for explanations, then you have a full life's work! The easier way is to use the Bible in classes, and to open your mind to the Brotherhood of God who is trying to teach you."

"What role do churches have in helping us find truth?" I asked.

"People who call themselves Christians give their open minds to the church to give them understanding. They think and discuss the church's wonderful contribution to Christianity. Then they tune out the true wonder—the God of their being who is there to fill them with power. They turn to the church to find answers, not to the God of the Universe. They think that the church opens their minds, not God. They think the church will bring them peace, thoughts of enlightenment, but they do not turn within. The truth is that the churches tune out God to the people. The God of our good is the same God of the Universe, but we do not understand the power that we can have over our lives. The God of the Universe is the One who gives us the true enlightenment, not the church."

This assessment of the role of churches seemed quite harsh to me because I'm a confirmed church-goer. I asked again about the churches, and asked if someone would like to qualify these statements somewhat. Here is the response. "The God of the Universe, the wonderful Goodness, is shut out when people turn to earthly truths such as the church's belief that God punishes us that we may become good. People turn to earthly good such as the fellowship to give them sustenance. But they go to the truth of the earth, not the truth of the universe. There is a powerful difference. The church people want goodness, but *they* define that goodness. They take the truth and twist it to make themselves feel they understand. But to really understand, they must go to the God of their being, to the God whose interest is to help them grow. This Brotherhood is the Counselor that Jesus promised to help this happen."

I asked about the new thought movement that has spawned many churches in this 20th century. "This new thought movement began strongly, but now it too has the beginnings of the dogmatic. The dogmatic is that which insists on ONE WAY to meet God—no other. Therefore, I tell you that there is no church free from erroneous thinking. God is here for all. No belief in a given church will get you in touch with the God of your being; only you can do this. "When the typing stopped, I asked if there was anything more on this subject. "This is the truth we tell here, the truth that gives God great power in our lives. God will give you growth, great power, joy—not the churches."

There must be value in churches, and I asked someone in the Brotherhood to state what this value is. "The value of our churches is that they give us program. They give us the opportunity to express our thoughts of the spirit to one another. They give ministers the chance to think the thoughts of the God-self and to promote those thoughts. The churches give people the opportunity to gain the spiritual enlightenment of the history of the Christian faith.

"The churches trouble us with dogma, of course. They lay guilt on us; they give us unrest. But they have certain value. If we can attend the church without taking seriously the overt attempts to bring us to the dogmatic viewpoint, then we can get something from church. Then we can exercise our own judgment without thinking ourselves hypocrites. The trouble with the churches is that the people who belong either think of themselves as hypocrites or as faithful servants. That way nobody comes out ahead. The dogma limits us, points us to our greater betterment but does not help us attain it. The church truth is the one people think up about God, but it is not God opening to our own beings. This God of Truth will come to all, but the churches try to limit our understanding of this by giving us the picture of the ONLY WAY to get to God.

"To have a better church, we must have no overt truth given. The way is to search the God-self by turning to God of the Universe. That way the truth will come to us individually, not collectively. There is the individual truth on the matter of God to consider. *There is no collective truth.*"

Astonishment at these words prompted me to ask if it wasn't fine to have statements—affirmations—like "God is all-good; God is all-powerful."

"These truths only grow into realities when they touch us individually. They can be repeated, but they mean nothing until they intrude themselves into our personal selves." I insisted that surely the churches can say these things as absolute truths. "They can and do, but there is no truth that reaches individuals until they go after that truth."

I tried to visualize a church service on Sunday morning with the minister or priest saying nothing to the people except to go find the God of their own being. What could those who lead the services say to people? "They can tell people that God is real, came a suggestion. "They can tell them that God gives them their truth, that God brings them to understanding. Then the minister or whoever may tell the people to go to the God of their own inner being to learn the rest."

I asked about collective readings and affirmations to help establish a mind-set. "The mind-set comes from God. The mind-set is the being's own work. Point to the growth—the plan of God in lifetime after lifetime. Then let people work out their true plan with God. The minister's job is to explain that people will not be alone in this work."

"Each Sunday the minister would say the same thing?" I asked.

Here my communicator gave specific suggestions. "The

minister's method may vary—meditation, music, the message of God-self discovered by others, the work of the advanced spirits in them, their opportunities to make the most of each lifetime. The minister can tell people the best truth is the truth that comes from within, and he can tell them that his truth is not theirs exactly, though theirs may be similar. He can tell them how to contact the Brotherhood/Counselor."

Why, I wondered, is one person's truth different from another person's truth. "Isn't TRUTH unchanging?"

"The truth that is unchanging is that God exists. The truth that varies from individual to individual is that which affects growth. The truth of my soul is not the truth of your soul. This is the true way to ascertain truth—that it is only for your own growth, not someone else's."

I asked about people who take strong stands on certain social issues and proclaim that stand as God's own belief. "This concept is indeed false. Those who feel strongly may ask if there are others who agree with their stand. Then they may proceed together to influence the opinions of others. But to enter their belief or their truth into the book as God's truth on the subject forever and for all is not the truth at all. That way they condemn all who differ from them. Theirs is the dogmatic way again with one person judging another."

I inquired about the value of inspirational books in our search for truth. "These open our eyes to the possibility that there is more than one truth abroad. The thing to do is to read, but try to find your own truth. This matter of taking the truth of someone else and trying to fit it into your unique life plan is NOT the thing to do. Books about religion that try to inspire us to connect our lives with God bring us much to contemplate. However, they must cause us to go to our own source of truth—God.

"Many books on religion give the truth as the writer finds it, and they try to put you into the same wave length. That is not the thing to do at all. Try to resist such things as the revealing of *One Way to God*. Take each suggestion, each method, each truth that the writer gives, and then put it into perspective. That perspective is your own viewpoint that is joined with the truth God has to give you. Take the truth to your inner temple to be remolded into your practical life. There in your inner temple will the truth be opened to you and to you alone."

What advice, I wondered, would those in the Brotherhood have for parents in the bringing up of their children? "Hopefully the child has come to the earth plane with a growth plan within the God-self, but the revealing of this plan is not always wonderfully clear. Therefore, people wander this way and that way, entering into various experiences to find the ones that will express their plan. But if they will go to us for help, we can help them understand their true growth plan.

"Not everyone, however, comes with a clear plan, but it is the parent's duty to help the child understand that though it is God's ideal to come with the plan intact, each person can still learn of this plan through prayer. When a person turns around in his thinking and in his actions, that probably means the plan has been received. Then that person turns away from emptiness to the light of God shining on a path. This is part of the parents' work, but no parent can guarantee success. The individual is responsible to the plan, to the lifetime, and to God."

When does the parents' responsibility to their children end? "The parents have the main responsibility of bringing the child forth to life, then to care for it and to love it. Then there is education, both truth and the historical education. When the responsibility is over, the parent tells the child, now grown, that he or she is the one to express his growth spiritually by way of truth messages that God has for each person. These messages will come to him or her from God through the Counselor/Brotherhood of God. 'This is the time,' the parent will say, 'that you must take responsibility for this life you have come here to live. This life is your plan made with the help of God before you were born. This is the truth that will give you the point to the living of your life. Be happy,' you will say to your child now grown. 'Take your God-self to the Brotherhood to get the help you need. Then your lifetime will not be wasted. It will be fruitful and great.' "

I wondered if truth is hard to put into action. Deep inside me I supposed there must be suffering and misery on my part.

"This is the Brotherhood of God. This truth we speak of here is the truth that opens our eyes to the possibilities that God has to give us. This truth is not hard, nor is it that which causes suffering. Truth opens our hearts and minds to the joyous way of life, to the beautiful, to the perfect way.

"Truth—the truth of God. Truth—the one that comes to you with the help of our Brotherhood. Truth—that which wells up within us. Truth—that which is irresistible. Truth—the best that we know. Truth—that which brings us in touch with the God of our being. God the Truth, the Principle, the Wonderful Growth, the Good that is with us, the Good that works through us, the Being that encompasses the thought energy of the universe into that which is, that which exists, that which teaches us truth. Truth—that is the goal of your being on this earth."

CHAPTER 7

LEARNING MORE ABOUT THE NEXT PLANE OF LIFE

How can I use my thoughts to produce the good life — in the next plane of life as well as in this earth plane?

Those in the Brotherhood believe that we on this earth plane need to give consideration to the next plane of life before we go there. The better we understand the next plane, the quicker we will adjust. Those who go to the next plane with false expectations or with no expectations at all must go through a long period of re-education. "The God-self that you develop on the earth plane will give you good truth, but if you have not given thought to this plane, you will be in shock for awhile." It is to lessen this shock or to prevent it altogether that this chapter is written.

"Here on this plane our thoughts are expressed into things. Yes, in order to express these good things of life, we only need think of them."

Startled, I stopped the reception momentarily. "This is too confusing to understand, perhaps," the messenger continued. "But we would not get the things we need here unless we manifest them through thought. This way we think carefully, not wildly. We get our thoughts under control so that we can be on the mark to manifest what we need. If we miss the mark, we might manifest our fears, our goblins or our other horrors, and then we have a hell of our own making."

My conception of heaven was one of beauty and peace. I waited for someone to speak to this thought.

"The 'heaven' that you speak of is created from your mind. It isn't a permanent place in this plane where your spirit is sent."

"Then Jesus isn't 'preparing a place for me' that where he goes, I may go also?" How many times I have heard the Biblical Jesus quoted in this way!

My teacher quickly responded. "Never think that God takes charge of your spirit either here or there on earth. You enter free on this plane that you may choose to be one with God or not. This is the immutable law which God is. Do not enter into the idea that Jesus has the responsibility for where your spirit self will go in the next plane. Neither Jesus nor any of the Brotherhood herds spirits into heaven like sheep who must go where the shepherd makes them go. However, teaming up with Jesus or with other advanced spirits will give you more assurance that each person has a helper.

"If you will begin now to use your thought very carefully, you will be ready to direct your life when you come here. In this way you can learn to use your thought process for good, not bad. That you may understand this better, we might compare your present thought with any trouble you have. Trouble gives you pain, and you can either pray it away, or you can give it power so that you put the matter into concrete.

"The way to give yourself the good life is to concentrate on that which is good. To give power to evil is to give power to the concrete that weighs you down. Think instead of the opposite— the other side of the coin. If you first think, 'my illness is terrible,' change it about quickly to 'health is my true state.' Instead of thinking entirely of poverty, think of plenty, and be specific. What do you really need and want? Give these things your clear thought."

I asked if it is true that we can change our troubles into good experiences and our lacks to plenty? "That you should experience lack when you have the substance that never runs out is a matter of wonderment to us on this plane. Of course you can use this substance!"

I countered by asking just how this is accomplished. "The HOW is the matter of concentrating on the substance that is present, that is everlasting, that which gives energy to any creative thought. God gives us this substance to use, not to wonder at.

"The first thing to do is to get your thoughts under control. Then focus on the great supply of God that is open to you. There is no lack, no limit to this supply. There is so much that it is impossible to deplete it. Therefore, reach forth to claim that which you desire. Your desire tells the substance that you are thinking the thought that will open the supply to you. Then you energize this thought by giving it to the God of your being, the One who has your best interests in mind. This God will never fail you. He is the plentiful good Father who tries always to lead you in the path you have chosen to accomplish your soul growth.

"The second thing to do is to hold the idea of what you want in your mind. Think it in detail, think it in its every aspect, think it to the point that you know you see it clearly. Then feel the joy you have because of this tremendous true worth that is given you. Be open with the truth that God gave the gift. Use it with the abandon of the rich who know there is more where this gift comes from. Understand? The Father is that which expresses in many ways, but He is the rich Father. This concept is the belief that God is what He claims He is—the Giver of all Good, the True Wonder that in this world manifests what is needed by the ones who accept His promise."

If we are to manifest our good thoughts, those in the Brotherhood say we must choose to go along with truth. Otherwise, we will cling to the old ideas that keep us buried in the wayward thinking of belief in a God Who empties His wrath upon us. "It is time," my communicator says, "for new thoughts."

"The thought process is the main thing here in this plane. If people do not accept it, they begin to believe they are crazy or weird. This idea of thought manifesting is the thing to accept." I suggested that earth-bound souls who have passed on to the next plane of life must not understand this principle. "The earth-bound ones want to live again on the earth. They still have their earth problems with them. They cannot let go. They manifest their agitated thoughts into the belief that they will be doomed to hell. They feel unworthy and their thoughts create unworthy conditions."

I asked for an example. "The spirit of one person came here without instruction as to the thought process. The thoughts of this person were of the guilt of sins thought unforgiven. These guilt feelings brought the person into sad circumstances—the poor house to hide in, the poor truth to give him comfort, the great fear of judgment that hung over him to be his greatest heartache. This person believed God had a poor opinion of him and therefore the person created poverty around him because he thought he deserved it.

"Then we began to instruct this person that God holds the truth for each individual, and that he must find the truth by searching his own inner being. But it is so hard here. There is no life expressed except what that person has made. The entity has no material world to come up against. And there is no worthy person in his environment to demonstrate a different truth. All a person has is the environment he creates. That is the entire circumstance to this person, and there he stays, fixed in concrete."

"You mean," I asked, "that people who think of themselves as 'a poor miserable sinner' create the misery that you described?"

"This is our truth," came the answer, "that you will create here on this plane whatever picture you have of your being. Therefore, it is important to become a lover of your own soul, to be a person who tells yourself worthy thoughts. Tell yourself that you are lovable, that you will attract good. Then with this mind-set you will come here ready to create the beautiful and the good and to point your way to the best that growth can produce."

I asked if this same truth could be applied to our lives in this earth plane. "This same truth is true on the earth plane. That you may understand that you create your own world even on earth, look around you. That you have created your own true growth in your surroundings is quite evident."

They noted specifics in my life such as my husband whom they called my "perfect mate," my home, its furnishings. Then they added, "These things are purely material. There is no spiritual value that will make them the wonderful and entirely good thought-things that you will take here. They will vanish from your life. That is all right, for you do not care much for material things. But for those who think they must 'take it with them' in some way, they need to clothe their valuables, their precious things in this thought-energy that will be the spiritual reality."

Now here was a brand new concept—that we can "take it with us" when we leave this plane. They were right when they said I do not care much for material things, but there are always those special items that I, too, would like to take with me—at least until I outgrow the need of them.

I asked again about producing our desires from this substance that is unlimited and versatile. "If you need food, you can produce food. You may need other things, and you may produce them too. When you wish for things you cannot afford with earth currency, turn to the substance." I had the feeling of offhandedness here as if the matter of turning substance into whatever we desired was a simple matter. Also, I received the definite impression that these advanced Brothers wonder at my own denseness that I must spend so much time discussing the concept. In some exasperation, I thought, one wrote, "Accept this as we give it to you. That is all you can do because there is nothing in the material that can possibly tell you how this works. This is the truth we give you. Try to enjoy this truth without taking it apart. That is the way to enter new truths into your mind: do not take them apart; accept them."

I believe various Brothers answer my questions. For when I returned to the subject of the substance yet again, I received a more patient answer. I mentioned that there are many materially rich people on this earth plane who have created beautiful homes and furnished them lavishly. I asked if these people have these things because of their own self-worth.

"That you may understand this concept, let us teach you the principle with more detail. The pure substance that you have available is that which you attain without sweat. That which you sweat to earn is that which is created the material way without the substance of God entering into it. There are two kinds of manifestation, you see. One is by the sweat of the brow, and the other is from the substance of God. But on this second plane of life there is only the substance, not the material. That is the big difference. So what one thinks of himself may affect his life there on the earth plane as far as material possessions are concerned, but this is not the entire point. The substance makes material things glow with the reality of spirit, and it contains the promise that God is the giver. The open channel that gives you this truth trusts you to understand this concept. The entire point here is that you endow the things you own by giving them the reality that God has to give you. That which is the truth will not perish, but that which is material substance will perish."

When those from the Brotherhood speak of reality, they speak of spirit. When we on this earth plane speak of reality, we are most likely to point to material things. Bringing these two realities together on this earth plane is our task if we indeed want to make our individual worlds beautiful and eternal.

"The entire point of what we say is to give you the understanding that God is the true giver, not man. That material things *think* is not unreasonable. That the thought gives them reality is to clothe them with the great power that is of God. That is the way that you can 'take it with you,' you see. Clothe your things with the spiritual substance of God which is the reality we deal with on this plane of life."

I suggested that it is not easy for me to accept this concept of the spiritual substance, for I live in a world that uses money as the means of attaining things. Everything was manufactured or made by hand. They have a solid appearance. They are real to me as they are.

"These solid matters give the impression of eternal truth, but they perish and decay because they are subject to the earth opinion. The earth opinion or thought is that matter decays. The opinion of this next plane of life is that there need not be decay. We make the things we need, give them their solidity, but if we no longer want or need them, they fade away. The things you have there open themselves to your thought energy that there is decay, so they decay. They give themselves to God's pure substance again. That is what decay is—going back to the pure substance from which they came. That is the truth.

"Wood is supposedly solid and is made into furniture. But it is not the solid that it appears. The solid is only the appearance. The only solid aspect is the wonderful truth that we can alter its shape, its exterior. But the part that holds it together is the joining of complex elements that hold fast. But even they are not stable enough for eternity. These elements require petrifying, that we do with our thoughts, to make this substance permanent. We call forth the true God-substance to be energy that zeros in on the needed reality—that which is incorruptible, that which is inoperable, that which is inviolate, that which will not decay or pass away. The petrifying is possible when you think of the wonderful power of God to clothe these things in His great energy. Then the things will be as if petrified. They become lasting and they can be taken with you to the next plane because they are already thought-forms."

Frankly I was overwhelmed by these truths. There is no way I will ever look at my world in quite the same way as I have looked at it before. I remember my first chemistry class in college when the subject of the elements of the universe was first presented to me. I learned the formulas of many substances I used daily—water, air, and many others. The truth that came from the professor of chemistry was that there is no such thing as solid matter. I always felt much wiser about my world because of the chemistry course, but until I received these truth lessons from the Brotherhood, I had never given these facts the serious attention they deserve.

I asked about the other aspects of life on the next plane. People always wonder if they will see those they love on the other side. Some wonder if their lives will continue in much the same way with appreciation for the arts or nature, or creative endeavors. People are so different from one another. Lifestyles differ. Will there be a feeling of being at home in the next plane?

"I have the law of the next plane of life ready to give you. Be open to the idea that though the principle described is the wonderful truth that is here, the picture is not entered into your understanding. Therefore, it is not possible on your plane to understand the picture that I give you. But we will try together anyway. This is the Brotherhood of God reporting this to you.

"This plane is pure thought-form here. The environment is thought. Outside of our spirit bodies, we give the rest of the environment that which we have inside ourselves. We express here according to our growth. That means that we enter into one another's good truth if we on this plane find it compatible with ourselves.

"The ones who join together here have much in common, you see. There must be this common thought to maintain the loveliness we wish to live in. Then there is the matter of getting along together. We abhor friction. Therefore, we gather around us those who believe in the same pattern of thought as we do. Then we on this plane become one in our thought process. That way we build what appears to be solid matter—the trees, the homes, the waterways etc. But it is all thought manifested according to our mutual growth patterns. This way we have no time spent on bickering. We trust one another completely. There is no time spent on worry over our health, for we all think ourselves into perfection of our bodies. There is no time spent on the on-stage opportunities to make ourselves powerful because there is nothing here that power can mold or can manage. Only the mutual thought waves bring the power that provides our good.

"This is not worrisome. Don't think we live in an unstable environment. Entities who know and understand how to express God truth team up to bring their own good to one another. That way they create a stable environment.

"The unstable environment is possible, however, if entities of unstable thoughts gather together. They give their mutual instability to one another and thus create what they think.

"On your plane there are those today who will bring their weaknesses to this side to re-enact the picture here that they keep insisting is their truth—the weakness of the body, the weakness of the mind, the emotions, the constant peculiar growth patterns that they have. Then they group together with others of like mind who hold to the idea that their home is made up of bad, of evil, of ghastly fears, of problems that beset them. When they fix their minds on these negatives, they think their own environment into existence—troubled weather, power-seeking brothers who tell them what to do and what to think. They hide themselves in this environment hoping they will emerge from it when they become worthy.

"The truth of their place of habitation is that they believe their way is the only way, the right way, the best way to God. They take themselves to the truth of their own making. They take themselves away from open minds. They close themselves in this cloister of unhappiness just as they did on earth. Oh, they do not know they have done this. They think they must be in heaven, and the fact of survival is enough for them to call it heaven. To reach them with the story of inner truth is like going to the bottom of the ocean to tell the deep sea fish the truth of the God-self. They would keep on opening their mouths, never listening, never heeding your words. They have closed minds, closed hearts."

I asked if any of these people with closed minds and closed hearts are religious people. "They think they have religion, for they think they have the seal of God upon their beings. They peek out now and then and believe that we in the beautiful atmosphere must be on the road to hell. Their idea of heaven is that it is hard, that it is God's wish that they be as they are. They believe in the God of the judgment, not the God of the Universe."

"So," I commented, "some of our earthly friends may elect to cling to one group and some to another."

The Brother answered, "This is right, of course, but those on this plane who love one another will be together. It is God's law that love brings us together. The law or principle here is that the only bond worth growing is true love."

"You described two kinds of environments there on your plane," I reminded my communicator. "People have various kinds of belief systems, so there must be many more environments."

"The belief systems you speak of become the growth patterns here. Then together people use thought to belong to their own growth pattern. That way the various atmospheres become the 'home base.' People can travel to see the other places, but they may not interfere. They may observe, but there is no missionary work here. There is no thought going out to change anyone, for on this plane it is difficult to grow for the reasons you can plainly see."

I came back to the subject of our souls grouping themselves into various patterns. I asked for further enlightenment. "There is no problem. The growth patterns just group together into clusters like the chemistry you study on the earth plane explains the grouping of atoms and molecules to form matter. We touch the ones we open our minds to. That way we find true homes here. That way there is no trauma over the judgment and so forth. Even the criminals, the hideous minds that touch one another on your plane can touch one another here and believe they have found heaven—for awhile at least. The 'at least' refers to their possible growth. They will grow dissatisfied with their lot and begin to let their minds open up to truth. They may drift away from this first group to cluster with another group. This way no one is teaching, but all here learn as they can. This is why it is so important on the earth plane not to waste the lifetime, to learn the lessons, to be the open channel—the Christ that communicates to us to learn the truth and to re-connect with God."

The Bible pictures God as our judge, and I asked someone to comment about this. "The God of judgment is the one that everyone knows for sure. This God is known because we all subscribe to the need of judgment to bring the justice we think is deserved. This God of judgment is that which gives us our inner conviction on the way we live our lives. This God of judgment tells us the truth in the matters that contribute to the growth of our being. But we do not grow into God's good persons by knowing ONLY this God of judgment. This judgment is only the primary, the first step into self-knowledge. This God of judgment gives us the power to tell that we enter the wrong path, to open our eyes to truth, to be there to warn us. To go on from there, we must be open to the other truths that God has to give us."

"I read in the newspaper yesterday that 42 children died in a bus accident in South Africa," I told my communicator. "I have been thinking about the shock, the fear, the trauma of these children as they died. What happened to them?"

Here is the reassuring answer. "These children awoke on the other plane without remembering anything of their death. Death is a brief thing. It seems to be a long thing, but it is not in actuality. Death is not an awesome thing, and the circumstances are even forgotten here. These children here with us give their attention now to their real identities, their true selves. They touch the growth pattern they feel most comfortable in, and they go home—home being that place where they are most comfortable."

I asked if any of the children were waiting around to see their earth families. "They may, but few do this. Only those who have no truth to sustain them in the matter of the touching of the growth pattern. They fear it all, these earth-bound ones. They withdraw into themselves."

Returning to the subject of the clusters of souls who think alike, I asked again about their social life. "Social life is one thing to you, but this social life you speak of is not the same here. This plane is thought. In this plane there is an openness that you on the earth plane cannot comprehend. Therefore, getting together for conversation is not needed. Our thought travels out to those we wish to speak to and others pick it up too. To wish for companionship is to have it. To want music is to have it as there are many involved in music. To want to see art displayed, well—that is everywhere because artists beautify our entire environment. They touch all of us with their beautiful thought-designs—paintings, sculpture and other pure beauty.

"There is theater, of course. This, too, touches the lives of those who love to wander in the time of the past or the growth truths or the God-self manifesting. The theater gives us much to interest us in the forward movement of our lives here. There is no pornography here because there is no audience for it.

There may be such an audience among some clusters. There are poor souls that cling to all their lusts even though they cannot satisfy them. This is the saddest group of all."

I asked if there was anything else those from the Brotherhood wanted to explain about the next plane of life. "The next plane of life is your true home, of course. This plane gives us the best that our minds can think of. This plane is the wonderful place you make it, or it is the terrible place you make it according to your own thoughts of yourself. Be the one to create good by thinking good. Think good of yourself and of those you come into contact with. Think the best in them to manifest that best. Give your heart to God, to the God of your being who is the all-good principle."

CHAPTER 8

"Nothing real can be threatened; nothing unreal exists." Miracles

WORKING OUT OUR DESTINY

How can I progress spiritually and at the same time make my dreams and ambitions come true?

"God is real. God is practical. This idea that God is an impractical concept like pie in the sky is ridiculous. The reality is God, for that which is of God does not perish, rot or fade away. What in your earth plane can take that challenge? What else can that be said of?"

This chapter contains much that staggers our minds, that causes us to blink in disbelief, but which gives us hope that our best thoughts about God are really true.

"Give attention to your hopes and dreams, and give your ego to God, to His substance, to His true being which is the growth. Then speak the word that you receive. God is filling you with truth that is specifically for your own being, truth that will bring you understanding. When you believe you have been filled with this truth, you will be one with God in your purposes.

"Give God each picture that comes to mind that he may purify it." The picture refers to that desire or need which you hold in mind. "Then take the picture he has refined to your inner being for safekeeping. This picture will spring forth into the manifestation of what you have pictured with God's help. This way you and God together will be working out your destiny. Take the pictures—the plans, the hopes, the expectations of the life you want to live—and present them to God."

As I reread the above material, I followed the instructions. I pictured my deepest dreams and ambitions, my hopes and expectations. They seemed illuminated with a very bright white light. "This bright light," one of the Brothers told me, "is illumination that comes to you from God. Let these pictures bask there in this light without haste in their development. Know that God is working to refine the pictures even now. Those pictures you wrote down earlier, those you think you want in your life, these are the ones He takes to His truth.

"The best part of the process is that it works. This process always works. Take no thought for the outcome until God refines this picture. Then be the open mind to receive them back refined to their perfection. They will delight you. They will satisfy you. They will be the heart's desire you think not to express for fear of being too thankless or too unworthy. There is this 'plenty' in the universe with which we can deal. This 'plenty' has nothing to do with the outer things you see, but is of the invisible, the invisible that will bring forth the many dreams we have when we give our pictures to God for development."

No doubt the matter of our thoughts becoming material by our use of the belief factor and the universal substance gives all of us much pause for concern. Even if we could, *should* we be doing this? Is it witchcraft? Is it a selfish evil impulse? Is this dangerous or self-deluding?

"That we could be your teachers of evil is unthinkable," came the swift answer. "There is no opportunity that has come to mankind that he has not resisted if the idea was new. The opportunity is now given to these readers to try for themselves these truths that have their basis in the truth of God of the Universe. This truth is not just pointing toward our own plane, but it points to yours too. This truth gives ways that can solve many of the world's problems. That we would give untruth is laughable. This Brotherhood is incorruptible, for it is created by the spirit of God.

"This truth is that which God wishes to impart. It is not hidden, it is tuned to your wave length, it is the thought-energy that opens the mind to all that God has to give. Not many understood this when Jesus was on earth. Not many understand it today. God wants to give good gifts. This God of the Universe wants to bring everyone into His understanding, to bring them close to Him in the way of using the truths. This is our mission here—to bring the truths. Then you and God together bring the truths into manifestation.

"Then there is the matter of thought becoming material by using the God-principle involved. Manifestation of thought always seems to those in earth life rather ridiculous, but it too works in a practical way if we will follow the principle involved. This principle has the elements of God, the universal God, plus the elements of your growth. Take the highest concept of God that you have, polish it brightly in your mind so that it shines forth. Nothing will hide it and nothing prevents the manifestation when there is the element of truth involved. You, plus the polished visualization of the highest concept of God, plus the truth that there is this substance in the universal to use, make the manifestation complete. Try it.

"Present your dreams, your hopes, financial needs, veteran thoughts that have been with you for the betterment that you see." I had to admit that these "veteran thoughts" were hidden so deeply within me that I no longer knew them. Whereupon a Brother listed those deep-seated hopes and dreams of mine, much to my surprise and delight. I suppose I had consigned them to the impossible-to-attain file and put them out of my mind.

"These wants are not selfish nor are they unattainable. Think not to test God, but to test yourself. You won't receive what you think you don't deserve. Therefore, open your mind and open your heart to God's wonderful goodness. On this side of the open channel we see you enjoying all that you desire in your heart. Be true to these thoughts. Open your mind to them to become real in your life. The point of all this is that people try to work through to their goals without taking God into the partnership. It is possible to bulldoze your way through, but the way to enjoy the whole thing and to have it meaningful is to put them into God's care and into His great power to manifest them."

I wondered if I should ask God to refine these rediscovered dreams. "This has been done," my communicator assured me, "and you know this because the pictures remain as they have always been. God has clarified them and held them out to you to bring the hopes into concrete. This is the time to polish them brightly because they are already God's highest thought in your life expression. Take them to your inner being knowing that God has them taking form in the outer.

"This business of truth turning our minds to practical work is the important concept to understand here. Our own inner truth frees us from the worry of taking many truths out and continually sorting through them. Your truth is yours only. This is our point here. Do not worry over other people's truth, no matter how they try to change or convert you. You and God work out the truth of your being. Then you will always walk in the light of God's sun." I asked if the word was "Son"— meaning Jesus—instead of "sun."

But there was no mistake. "No. The sun of which we speak is the illumination that God gives us all. The Son of which you speak is the relationship between God who loves us and our Christ selves. The sun of which we speak is not the relationship, but it is the pure light of God that shines on us when we turn our spirits to Him on matters of our soul growth."

Is religion simply turning to God for our truth? I checked out my definition with the Brotherhood's correspondent. "The definition of religion is that men and women will trust the God of their being to guide them into the life-path they will follow. Growth is of God, not of man's dogma. God is the One, the Power, the Pure Growth that we long for. Then religion is a matter of taking this inner truth to the turnabout that gives us our freedom to be ourselves, not reproductions in the church's machinery."

Life offers us many challenges, many decisions, many paths. How can we use truth to help us with these day by day choices and crises? "To become one with God we must first be one with our own growth pattern—the plan that God and we together build for our lifetime. Then we meet the challenges that come always with this inner truth bearing on all decisions, on all matters that pertain to our daily lives."

Over and over those in the Brotherhood speak of becoming one with our growth-pattern. I asked for a concise explanation of how we become one with that plan. "This is the plan in three parts. Take the true self, or God-self image you understand. Team up with God. Then be one with Him."

Like all concise explanations, there is a need for further explanation, and here it is. "To be God's true person, we must get in touch with His good plan that will help our lives to progress. In that way we arrive at the understanding of how to use the energy that pours to earth on command. This command is the law that is enacted when we become one with our God-plan or growth-plan. To enact our plan we must be one with it. To make use of the energy that will bring the plan into manifestation, we must be the true persons of God who empty ourselves of ego that God may fill us."

Obviously there is what we might call a natural law concerning our ability to live our lives according to our divine plan and the powerful energy that pours in for us to make use of. I asked why this energy comes only under these special circumstances.

"The reason is that the energy is the open channel's truth pouring through. Only those who tune into it, those who realize that they are on the right path will take this energy to use. The others rely on their own egos, their own promises to themselves. They do not look outside their egos to find this energy."

I asked for examples. "This example may be found in the creative arts where people speak of their illuminations or their inspiration. Then you know they have received this energy from the open channel into their hopes and dreams to enact their growth pattern. They draw from this source as naturally as the water goes downhill on the earth plane. They turn to God's sun—illumination, substance—to be filled."

I asked about business matters—making a living, providing financial security for ourselves and our families. "Then you must give thought on the matter to the open channel. In other words, the picture, the goal or course of action you want, must be refined by God. If it returns to you, then draw on this substance. This takes place rapidly—like thought. We have explained this process step by step so you may understand how it works."

Six months into this project between the Brotherhood and me, I was asked to put my mind in neutral and to try not to force anything at all. "Try to be in tune with our tone. To do this try to hear the right sound, the tone we give you. Try to put your mind into this neutral place and focus on the sound. The sound, the sound, the sound." The reason for this unusual beginning was to prepare me to receive information that I would find hard to believe. "This sounds very fantastic to those on earth because you have no way to relate to us in these matters. Try to believe without understanding so that you can grasp the concept."

In this way I entered into the day's reception and into a concept that I finally, with mental and emotional struggle, have come to accept. "The growth that is made lifetime by lifetime is the way to tell how a person progresses. To progress is to grow. To grow means living many lifetimes. To live these lifetimes, people must enter life through the woman's womb. But there may be some who enter the life plan by another route. These may come through the means of using the body that others on this earth are done with for one reason or another.

"Giving up a person's body to another is the right of the one giving it up, the right of the person who no longer wishes to live on the earth plane. Therefore, he or she gives up the body to become spirit. Another spirit who wants this body takes it over and continues the life experience. The one who comes into this body has a new plan, new energy, and a great consuming desire to accomplish the plan. At this point that particular human life begins to change for the better.

"This person holds the same memories and the good ties with friends and loved ones. Therefore, the new person gives us the true personality that was expressed before but with refinements. The refinements on the new personality are the soul's truths interposed there. In that way the person who is coming in may go ahead with the life.

"These persons who re-enter in this manner try not to disturb anyone. They become the beings that try to mold others into new creatures free of dogmas, free of fears, free of superimposed beliefs that obscure their own spiritual values. They touch the life of this earth in better ways than the first owner of the body, and this new owner has more impact upon the general growth.

"This is practical because sometimes people want out—really want out of this lifetime. They either commit suicide or they give themselves up to the great reluctance they have over living. In other words, they either kill themselves or they kill their growth-plan. Either way is not good, of course. It is much better to step aside and give your body up to another soul who will use it for good. This is easy to do. Just decide it, first. Then await our help to enact it. There will be a time set for the change, and there usually is a dream to indicate the exchange. Then there is a mere shuffling of spirits to make the exchange perfect. Certainly this exchange is much better than killing oneself or trying to live miserably—enduring, but not growing. Giving up your body to another is like giving a brother human being a transplant.

"These new personalities or souls will be the ones who advance quickly to the execution of their plan. They will be helpers to the rest of the people. This is an opportunity to put your body to great use in its entirety, not piece by piece after death. Think on this plan. Then instead of great despair taking you out of the earth picture, let another spirit take over. Your body-personality will continue and prosper and become the worthy thing you would wish it to be. Never worry over children nor over other concerns, for the new soul is as committed as you to all these responsibilities. Therefore, you can let go of your body without fear.

"This concept is the best plan we have here to use the advanced souls who can bring more peace to the earth plane. These persons can be the ones to bring new knowledge and wisdom to bear upon earth affairs. They will be the ones to lead people through difficult times."

I had read Ruth Montgomery's book, *Strangers Among Us*,* in which she outlines this same plan with many examples and details. Little did I know at the time I read her book that I

*Fawcett Crest Book, Published by Ballantine Books, 1979.

would ever be receiving a similar description of a process in which one soul gives up a body to a second soul.

I asked how the second personality is chosen. The explanation this advanced spirit gave me is that the second and first persons are basically of the same growth-pattern (belief system). That same attraction that clusters us together in the next plane of life brings the replacement for the first soul. Therefore, there is compatibility.

Certainly I agreed with the Brotherhood that giving up the body to another soul is preferable to suicide or a failure of the God-plan which could bring misery not only to the personality, but also to friends and family. Though the concept is hard to believe, I must accept it for I am one of those who came to this body in its mature years. When those in the Brotherhood informed me of this change, this re-entry to life through this body, I did indeed resist it. Though I knew I had changed in recent years, I tried valiantly to find plausible reasons for these changes.

Since a second soul enters the body and retains that body's memory, I am not aware of any specific time when this happened. However, I do know I hit a low period in my life. I felt terrible most of the time, and life hardly seemed worth living. I suffered from depression, and I longed for the past instead of finding joy in the present. One day I became aware of a new optimism and a keen interest in my life. I "knew" sugar was bad for me, and I began to cut down on my intake. Later I discovered I have diabetes, and I researched the disease, determined to control my blood sugar with diet only. I developed a sudden interest in playing a small musical instrument and was drawn to the recorder, a 14th and 15th century instrument. Many people have asked me how I knew of it, why I wanted to play it. I have no answer that satisfies me or anyone else. I simply "knew" the recorder was an instrument I wanted. And of course there is this new writing. One close friend pointed out certain changes in me, and my husband wondered aloud if I am the same person he married.

Various Brothers explained this re-entry this way. "The truth is that the one to occupy the body, your body, is not the original person who came in the day of birth, but a new soul, the new one who wonders if she can fulfill her mission here to write this book. This is why you came there. This is why you wanted to be on earth. The one I speak to now is that person, that new person. This is truth."

Stunned, I let the writing continue, hardly knowing what was written. "You bring your best self into this body-personality to enlarge its scope to better use. To become the best that you can be, you came into this body to try to work out new growth and to be open to our help. This you have done. This you have been." I asked when this transfer took place. "It happened one day while you were napping. That day you were discouraged, blue, depressed. Then you rose a new person. You were inhabited by a new soul—we talk to the body here. That day you knew to bring forth new hope, new growth, new God-life."

I had many questions, of course, like where is the other soul that inhabited this Jean Foster body. "That is the powerful thought that comes to your mind now and then to become the best wife to Carl that you can. That spirit is here, watching, cheering you on. This person is happy over the matter. This person gives you greetings here on your life there. This person has no thought of jealousy. She goes forth to be her own person, you see."

I asked the inevitable earth question, "Which of us will be Carl's wife on the next plane?"

The Brotherhood probably smiled in concert as the answer came. "That is not the great problem that you see it to be because here there is no love and marriage in the way of sexual love between man and woman. There is only the matter of this true self."

One of the Brothers tells me there is a difference between the way I love my husband and the way the first soul loved him. "She loved to the point of self-sacrifice, and you love to the point of trusting your own God-self more than you trust your husband."

Apparently I lay down one day despondent and miserable, and I got up glad to be alive and full of hope. I do know there has been a change. I know I am less dependent on my husband for my happiness. He must be relieved that this is so. I have new interests, and that I am well most of the time. I feel a deep contentment about my life.

The changes in my life came about gradually. Many times I felt that I—my mind—was training my body to become more mental and less emotional. My source said advanced spirits reached into my being with the understanding that the first soul need not suffer in the way she was doing, so I—the body— became available. "Then you—the soul—entered. Then the situation that caused the despair straightened itself out. You brought peace to that body, to that marriage, to the entire household."

Later I asked about the life readings they gave me earlier, and I wondered whose they were. "These life readings that you refer to are your own readings. The body has nothing to do with life readings. This is not a physical matter but a spiritual matter."

The questions that arose in my mind seemed unlimited. Would I, could I, ever accept all this re-entry information as truth? I learned that since the brain has recorded the earth life, I have memories that seem real to me. I am still the loving mother, the eager grandmother. I appreciate my husband's goodness, and I marvel at his unusual stability and good humor. I love him.

I asked if anyone in the Brotherhood had anything more to say on this subject. "True growth takes place by living many lifetimes. But there is more than one way to enter the life plan here. One is by birth, the other is by re-entry when the first soul is tired of life, suicidal, without hope in solving problems. Then it is time to relinquish the body to another who will take on the problems and solve them. This new person will take the thought of this plane with him or her and put the process of getting our help into practice. The second one will fulfill the first one's responsibilities and troubles will melt away. Then that soul will perform the task for which he or she came to earth. The business of the open channel being the contact is fresh in the God-mind of the second soul, and that soul will move faster toward the truth. Then will come the true purpose, the pure untroubled substance that God has for those who wish to manifest."

It has not been easy for me to share the personal part of this concept because it's difficult to let go of personal ego and pride. "What will people say?" I ask myself. "Will my friends think I am strange?" And finally, "What will my family think of me?" My teacher/counselor says that I am an honest woman, and I have a responsibility to those who read this book to tell this personal story. Now it is told.

The Brotherhood's messenger summed up the subject of re-entry. "The truth of our being is that we come to earth to enact a particular purpose. Then we give up our bodies either to death or to another person who comes to enact a separate purpose. Either way—birth or re-entry—it is better that we have the opportunity to try again and again. This engendered growth (growth that is brought into being) is the best that is possible.

"To understand re-entry, one must begin to accept the pure love of God that gives us these many chances to become one with Him. To fully accept the truth of this re-entry, be into the thought of God that unifies the truth of our souls. He gives us more of Himself in each growth advance. He wants us to be one with Him even as Jesus was and is one with Him. This oneness is possible, not improbable.

"This oneness, the optimum potential expressing fully, gives us the pure understanding that empties us of the personal ego and gives us the pure truth by which we live. Then we open our eyes to all the universal truth, the great openness of God which gives us unlimited freedom of expression. There is nothing else that we can call this pure oneness with God except pure freedom to express the wondrous things that are then within."

CHAPTER 9

STANDING ON THE PROMISES OF GOD

What are God's promises, and how do I collect on them?

Those in the Brotherhood assure us that God's promises in regard to our earth lives and our eternal lives are true and reliable. But like any promise, nothing happens unless those who receive the promise step forward to collect it. We have a choice. We can go directly to God or we can ask for help from the Brotherhood who will show us the way to collect on the promises.

"God is the open door when we touch Him directly. But many have problems going directly to God, you see. They *want* to be one with God, but they *fear* Him too. And fear keeps them parted from the One who wants to be united with them.

"Take the matter of becoming more open-minded, for example. The God of the Universe has a message of hope within Him, but many who profess to know Him will not approach Him to get the message. They stand afar and throw their glances this way and that. They tear the teaching of God into shreds on the matter of being one with Him. They tell themselves that God thinks they are unworthy or they are too evil. They have no confidence in their immortality. They believe in the body. They believe in the material. They believe that God is too far away and disinterested, too great to give them their needs. Therefore, they turn away sadly. For that reason Jesus said there is a Counselor, the Holy Spirit, who will teach you and comfort you and free you from the misunderstandings between you and God."

The Brotherhood has listed many promises that we can collect on if we open our minds to the potential that each of us has to be one with God. As these advanced spirits said, we can go directly to God to have these promises fulfilled, or we can ask their help.

"The first promise is that teaming up with the Brotherhood of God unites you with God's good energy. Yes, God will give you all the energy you can use to demonstrate your needs and your desires, and the Brotherhood will provide you the help to make all this happen. We give only what God Himself has for you.

"The second promise is that the alliance between you and the Brotherhood will produce the open channel that connects you to God. This communication with God provides the inspiration, the help, the hope for the living of your days and nights. The teamwork we will have will bring new ideas, new thoughts, new ways of getting what you need to enact your God-plan. Faith is needed in this relationship, for the counselors will work with each person who asks and who joins with us in the faith that we exist and will help.

"The third promise that God makes is to teach those who want instruction that He is the powerful being He has told us He is. This powerful God, this everlasting God of the Universe, tells you that His power brings you into control of your world, your lives, your inner selves. This powerful God takes you where you are and gives you the power to move your lives forward in great leaps and bounds. He will inspire you with thought-patterns that will forever give you the true strength that overcomes worldly problems, whatever they are. This is all possible when you band together with the Brotherhood which has only the best interests of each person at heart.

"The fourth promise concerns our hope for the things that will make life pleasant. *This God of the Universe promises you that you will have all that you need.* There should be no hunger, no illness, no traumas over lacks of any kind. God promises to provide for those who merge with this Brotherhood to manifest their needs. Each person may request the energy that will provide the substance to fulfill all needs. This substance is not an illusion, nor is the energy. This is a promise that works."

The Brothers indicate that erroneous thoughts produce lack, so the way to collect on this promise is to use thought correctly. In response to my questions, the answer came that we must get in tune with the God of the Universe if we are to receive the substance that produces the manifestation. I get in tune, I am told, by going to God with my spirit which is called my God-self.

However, getting in tune with God does not seem easy to me, so I turn to the counselors for help. "There should never be famine or even lack of proper nourishment if people will team up with us to learn the unlimited thought energy that God has for all his people," came the insistent follow-up to the fourth promise. "There is no lack. There is only the illusion of lack on the earth plane. Only erroneous thoughts produce lack. People misunderstand God's great gifts to the ridiculous point of blaming God for lack. God has the substance. Why not use it? Why not apply the law, the principle of manifestation?

"The fifth promise concerns the development of your own God-self. *The promise says that you can develop your personality so that it reflects goodness, power, and the enlightenment of a creative spirit.* Believe us, there is no way to count all our truths that will help each person accomplish his objectives. There is only happiness and good energy for those who work with the Brotherhood to be the persons they want to be.

"*The sixth promise assures you that you may learn your permanent goals in life—the goals of your soul, not the goals of your flesh.* New ideas may then emerge because you will understand where you have been in development, and you will know where you are headed. These new ideas that come from within will reflect these spirit goals, you see, and you are assured that you are on the right track in your growth pattern.

"*The seventh promise tells you that you will not miss the mark in this lifetime if you team up with the Brotherhood.* This promise opens your eyes, opens your heart, gives you your good. People who unite with us will judge their own lives and be satisfied with what they have learned and the growth they have made. This is the promise.

"*The eighth promise that God has made is that you can choose your own parents.* You enter earth life from this side by means of uniting your God-self with the body of the baby just before it is born. The soul chooses the parents and the new condition. There must be a reason why you chose these people, and there must be a reason why you chose this particular body. The Brotherhood is the means to understand why your soul made these particular choices for this lifetime, and they will help you interpret this action.

"*The ninth promise from God touches your inner self, your soul, with the power to develop your special talents.* The Brotherhood will help you to make the connection to God so that He can give you the energy that will combine with your talent. Therefore, turn to those who stand ready to enter into the expression of your hidden talents.

"The tenth promise assures us that we can become contributors to the earth's good. There is much that we all can do in our lifetimes to make this earth a better place. But many merely talk about the needs. Not many act to improve conditions. Therefore, *this promise says that God has the means that people can use to create the better life on earth so that all people will prosper and benefit.* This energy that God has will be loosed upon these projects if people learn how to direct that energy toward them. The Brotherhood will be the open channel to give you this means, to give you this truth.

"*The eleventh promise compels your God-self to energize your own gifts, truth, and thoughts into the things that people desire and need—things that bring forth the great good in their lives.* This promise is from God to everyone who will team up with the Brotherhood of God to learn how this promise is carried out. No person brings his good into manifestation without the energy that God has, that substance or product from which everything is made. Teaming up with these helpers makes this energy, this substance, work into the form that is the new expectation of the person's mind. This is God's true promise."

I asked at this point what the difference is between the fourth promise and the eleventh. The fourth one promises all that we need and the eleventh one promises all that we need plus all that we desire. They seemed much alike to me.

Here is the answer. "The fourth gives the promise that people will not be in need, that they will have what their bodies require. The eleventh promise says that people can manifest whatever they wish to manifest. The fourth promise is the promise that more people will accept. The eleventh promise is the one that is a step beyond, the step into the infinite God of the Universe who can do all things. When we embrace this concept, this truth, and enact it in our lives, we, with God, manifest our heart's desire.

"*The twelfth promise pushes you toward the truth of your being—that you become one with God eventually when you proceed to make your truth God-centered.* The open channel—the Brotherhood's good thought opening to each person—will bring the perfect union between God and the individual. This union assures you that your God-self will express in perfect freedom which surpasses the natural laws, and turns you to the thoughts-are-things understanding. This union brings you the deepest joy that souls can know, and is the ultimate in what people want. There is no other experience that may compare, no other condition that is the quality of this one. There is no possible comparison. To be one with God is to be the epitome of the truth in expression.

"*The thirteenth promise is that God will love you to the limit of your conception.* This promise calls for you to enlarge your conception of God, to give your own thought of God the great magnitude it deserves. The promise means that this wonderful love will enfold you inasmuch as the soul can get that picture in mind. The love of God is everlasting, but the person's ability to receive it becomes the problem. With the help of this Brotherhood, you may enlarge your own understanding and receive the benefits of that love in your life.

"The fourteenth promise belongs to certain special people whom God wants to reach with the story of the open channel's value. *This promise gives the ones who have disabilities the special understanding that God will make their life experience worth living, worth enduring, worth growing.* Teaming up with the Brotherhood will give these special people their understanding, their inner realization of what they will accomplish by this particular lifetime. When they team up with those who will help them, they will be rewarded by this understanding and enlightenment that will come into their minds.

"*The fifteenth promise assures you that you will have the empathy that you seek to give your lives meaning.* This empathy is the understanding that God is indeed with you in spirit, with you in understanding your trials, and with you to comfort you. This Brotherhood will open the minds of those who wish it that this promise will be fulfilled.

"*The sixteenth promise is that God gives His best to each of you, not to one or two here or there.* Many who call on God think He gives only to a few, but His promise is that He is with all. To believe, to have faith in this promise, you must team up with the Counselor/Brotherhood to receive the understanding that will enable you to receive God into your hearts.

"*The seventeenth promise assures you of an understanding God to whom you take your troubles.* People often think this God they honor is too good to give their problems to, but He promises that He will take them into His breast to give persons ease from their burdens. The Jesus Christ message said to come to him, all who were heavy laden, but the truth is that Jesus meant that you must give those troubles to God whose power will dissolve them, and re-create them into positive happenings. Unburdening your problems is the first step in trusting God. This promise of God is the one you need to understand in order to walk upright, not burdened down with care.

"The eighteenth promise belongs to those who try to do all things by the sweat of their brows. *The promise God makes is that He will make the path easy if people will let Him.* God intends to alleviate the hardships, the difficult trials, thoughts that empty your minds of hope. God will make the hopeless happy and the burdened think their life is beautiful. The Brotherhood stands ready to help attain this promise for each of you, that your life will be one of beauty and of happiness.

"The nineteenth promise opens the mind to opportunities such as the particular kind of writing that this writer is doing. *This is God's promise: to give you guidance, hope, and good thoughts.* The Brotherhood can open the mind of any person who comes seeking. If you wish, you can turn to this same kind of writing that this writer is doing. God promises to be here for each of you in a personal way. We who team up with God will help you to find that personal way most suitable for you.

"*The twentieth promise is the one that gives the greatest comfort to everyone. God promises each of you the gift of eternal life.* This life is not earned; it is promised. To have the assurance of eternity is to believe God is in charge, that He says what He means, that what He means is the truth. Eternity is certain and forever. Your soul lives on and on. The judgment has nothing to do with the survival of your soul. Your soul survives! This is truth, and the Brotherhood will help you with this assurance.

"*The twenty-first promise reveals the role of the Brotherhood as your teachers and helpers. The promise of God is that there is a Counselor, the one who recalls the teaching of Jesus and gives you even more.* This promise is enacted today through our communication here in this book. This promise is evidenced here. But each person may claim this promise individually. There will be no ignorance, no great gap of understanding for you who open your minds to us that we may fill them.

"*The twenty-second promise says that God gives each of you who can understand it the means to clothe your body and your possessions with the incorruptible spirit which gives them their enduring reality.* In this way you may take your own body and your possessions into the next plane. This promise takes much to understand, and most on the earth plane take no notice of its power. But with the help of the Brotherhood, this energy is put to your use to accomplish this indestructibility.

"The twenty-third promise is that which the world awaits. This promise begins where the others leave off, for it takes you into the next plane to belong to the God-self that you have brought into being. The Bible promises that God will be with you always, even unto the end of the age. But we say, *God will be with you always, even beyond the end of the age.* This promise from God is the FOREVER kind, the kind that you will not escape from even if you wanted to. God, the Great Giver, the Father, the Innovator, the Creator, the True Energy Principle, the Best Thought Known—this God is with you on and on. This God is the One to whom you turn to be the true God-self that is the person you want to be.

"We end the chapter on promises. That God is forever is the word that means what it says. That God IS comes to most as no surprise. That God and you make the most of every life is where the Brotherhood enters the picture. We help to bring you the energy, the truth, the understanding, that you on the earth plane will live well."

I asked if these twenty-three promises are all that exist. I was told there are more. In a subsequent book more will be given when they provide the material needed to understand the rest of the promises. The promises in Chapter 9 are the ones explained in this book.

Creation

CHAPTER 10

LOSING OUR IDENTITIES AND FINDING THEM AGAIN

Why did my spirit self choose to separate from God?

God is GOOD. All that God creates is GOOD. Furthermore, God is incapable of creating anything except good. These basic concepts the Brotherhood puts forth through God-mind form the basis of all understanding about God as explained in this book.

According to these advanced spirits, it is the touch of God-mind that wakes us to the truth that God has to give us. They say that touching this God-mind gives us much that we could not possibly know in and of ourselves. "(Even) this Brotherhood cannot get this truth except by God-mind," they insist. In this chapter, these teachers explain why the spirit entities departed from God-mind and went instead into earthly bodies to seek their truth.

"God, wondrous God, thought to make the universe a truly good place. Bright spirits moved freely in the vastness of the galaxies. These spirits had the power that was true, the power that gave them mastery of themselves. But many did not recognize this self-mastery as the epitome of truth.

"They believed that energy was withheld from them, so they decided to give themselves further mastery by experimenting with the beasts that they created on this earth.

Therefore, they entered into these beasts, indulging themselves in mating, in eating, in the outrageous idea that they
were indeed the masters of all. As a result, they became
trapped within these creatures. The nothingness that they became was absolute. They submerged themselves into animal
form and lost their ability to use the energy of the universe.
They were encased in these bodies, and they could not withdraw."

What kept them from withdrawing, I wondered. Was God
punishing them because they were disloyal?

Quickly came the answer. "The truth of the matter is that
God became the gentle one who tried to free these spirits, but
they pouted and entered completely into the body truth. They
wanted God to give them plenty of energy, forgetting that all
energy enters a spirit when that spirit reaches out for it. *The
mind is the key, not the generosity of God.*

"There was such an outcry! Such terrible confusion on
earth! The animals destroyed themselves in order to become
the free spirit-entities again. When they were free, they
thought the whole experience not so bad after all. They
laughed, and they united with other like-thinking spirit-
entities. They re-entered earth life in the same revolting way.
They threw away their divinity to become animals. At this
point, they teamed up to become the first earth-mind.

"Into this collective earth-mind they put their own truth.
They believed that the God of whom they were a part was not
the real God. They gave themselves more and more to the energy of their own making, to the mind of their own making.
The spirit-entities thus became encased in animal form, and
the only freedom came at their death. That is the way they
lived, losing more and more of their God-energy until they no
longer even considered the God of the Universe.

"The cries from earth were many. The outrage they felt at
their predicament was terrible. The thrust of their thoughts
was that they were not responsible. The God they thought up,
the 'God of whatever,' taught them nothing. The 'God of whatever' did not touch their lives. The God of their own creation
gave them no comfort, no thought to encourage them. They

believed they were abandoned, and gave themselves up to hopelessness.

"Because they gave themselves up to hopelessness, even their deaths no longer freed them. They thought they were trapped, no matter where they were. In this next plane of life their poor concept continued. They clustered together according to the growth-patterns they had developed, and they filled themselves with more untruth.

"Therefore, when they returned to earth, they went without plan, without hope. They returned simply to return—because there was nothing else to do. These persons encased within animals were the most miserable of the thought-forms on earth. They touched themselves with the idea that there was no other way. Therefore, they found no other way. Their thoughts on this second plane of life brought forth whatever they believed, you see. Therefore, they could learn nothing of the true predicament they were in.

"The God of the Universe touched their lives, however. This God, whose principle is goodness, urged the other spirit-entities to go to those on earth to reclaim them. Then came the creation of man, the wonderful creature with the brain that could use the God-mind available to all. This creature was beautiful beyond compare. The spirit-entities took these forms in delight. They worked to perfect them, to become the worthy thought-forms in expression. These true spirits brought order to the earth. They corralled the beasts that were inhabited by spirit-entities, those who had entered themselves in that debased fashion. The true spirits spoke to them and told them who they were in reality. The beasts listened, saddened by the truth, but nevertheless given hope for better times.

"They began to think differently. They began to understand the truth that they were really offshoots of the wonderful God of the Universe. They tried to improve their lot. They—man and beast—took concern over the creation problems. They took the truths they knew, established them upon the earth, and they began to separate man from beast. The God-selves that had inhabited the beasts began to leave—some by death, some by using the principle of truth."

At this point in the story, I fervently hoped that mankind began a positive chapter. However, those spirits that originally inhabited and then were trapped in animal bodies had not learned much. As those in the Brotherhood might say, they had developed no growth. They re-entered life again—this time as women and men.

"When they returned," my communicator continued, "they frolicked even more, having taught themselves very little, it seems. They even took themselves into the beasts to interlock with them and began a terrible turn of events—the mixing of the human form with the animal. This turn of events brought further entrapment. But those who entered into the offspring suffered beyond measure. The men and women brought them into subjugation, into slavery, into the position of not being able to reproduce. They had to make some of these creatures into men or women by taking the tails away or the tusk or the hoof, whatever it was that made the man less than man. But the principle was finally established that no person could mate with an animal. Then this species of half-human and half-animal died out.

"At this time the truth entered into the mind of mankind that the man/woman creatures were the truth of God implanted within the beautiful bodies. That recognition began the period of worship, but not the end of division—the division between people and God.

"The truth of all this story is that the spirit-entities that were one with God chose to leave this bliss to become creatures, and later to become the women and men of earth. These spirit-entities were the ones that taught the rest of the spirits that earth is theirs and the fullness thereof. 'This earth,' they said, 'is ours, not God's. This earth gives us our truth, our bounty, our sustenance. This earth belongs to us and gives us its abundance.' They appointed leaders. The leaders formed tribes. These tribes disbursed over the world. This time the poor truth—that the earth gave them everything—opened them to the earth collective mind and turned them away from the light that would have come through the God-mind."

It is at this point in the development of man, according to the Brotherhood, that recorded history begins. However, the

history of mankind's progress back to truth, back to the oneness with God, is recorded for the reader by the Brotherhood
through God-mind.

"Teaching that 'God the Thought' (an improved concept of
God) takes the truth to us finally turned the tribes toward the
light. This 'God the Thought' gave them hope of eternal truth
to help them team up with what was good, what was productive, what was true. They began to develop concepts of God
that grew into the various religions that cover the earth. They
took some light, they took some of their traditions, and they
took something from enlightened leaders. They put together
their religion—a belief system that encompassed what they
felt and what they thought.

"Their religion led them to express the God they knew in
gentle ways or harsh ways, depending on the tradition they
had. Each tribe wanted its religion to be dominant. That way
their truth was based on strength—the one who could outfight
the others became the most powerful. The powerful truth was
demonstrated by the powerful tribe.

"Women received a poor reception into these tribes because
they were not the wonderful warriors. Therefore, to enter into
life as a woman was the least desirable position possible. The
men and the boys were the ones who got the tender attention.
Strength was so important that old age and powerlessness
meant it was time for death by natural means or by killing the
old and the weak. These customs and others gave people order,
but it taught them nothing that would bring them into oneness with God.

"Then the God of the Universe sent enlightened spirits
among them to live. The tribesmen either had to deny what
they saw in the way of demonstration and by the way of example, or they had to accept the truth that was obvious to everyone. In this way the tribes slowly prospered in the truth.

"As truth began to manifest, the beginnings of true prosperity began—prosperity in growth, prosperity in the quality of
life, prosperity in terms of creativity. These changes took place
so that prosperity might demonstrate the God-mind in opera-
tion. This God-mind they began to tap took people into the
truth that would bring them oneness with God.

"The truth that people began to learn informed them that there is an open channel by which they may learn of the higher consciousness, this God-mind. Teaming up with the Brotherhood brought them into the open channel, the means by which they could unite with God-mind. This way people opened their minds to the truth that God had for them. Now the earth-mind began to diminish in importance, and the earth's people began to turn to God-mind for their wisdom, their truth, their beautiful thoughts.

"The God-self that had been so terribly distorted awakened to the possibilities. The entire earth awakened to beauty. The spirit-entities that inhabited the bodies enlarged their concepts of themselves, the God they worshiped, and their truth. God-mind led them to a burning ambition for goodness, in life, in beauty, and in music. At last they turned themselves toward the light. The truth of their beings teamed up with the Brotherhood to invade the entire earth.

"But not all was as smooth as it sounded. Power struggles continued as despots sought influential positions. Some turned toward the darkness of life as they turned back to the 'God of whatever' (a very poor concept of God) that made no difference in their lives. Nevertheless, life in general progressed. God-mind flourished once it found the light, and nothing could ever put it in total darkness again."

On this hopeful note, those who brought these words turned their attention to the present time, to earth life and the ever-demanding need of people to solve their problems. "People must understand the past in order to understand the present," one Brother began. "People must know the beginning of the spirits' troubles in order to understand the way to become free of them. This time of existence is the time of the CHOICE, a time for turning to the light or turning toward the darkness. To become one with God, there is only one choice—the light. There is no such thing as a *little* darkness. There is only the CHOICE between light and dark, between the purity of God or a troubled existence.

"A CHOICE exists because the God of the Universe opens our eyes to the truth so that we see more clearly than we once did. The truth brings us the entire spectrum of the brightness that obliterates the evil intentions that produce a troubled existence. The truth is obvious to many—that the CHOICE is ours today to use or misuse this plan of earth life. Earth life can become one with God—a paradise of a kind in material form. Or it can become the boiling cauldron of hate that solidifies the atmosphere and chokes life away.

"Truth begins in the truth that God IS. Truth finds roots in the beliefs of man and woman. Truth finds growth in the use of the powerful energy that God gives on request. Truth takes its sustenance from the practice of it by more and more of the God-selves that inhabit the human bodies. This tremendous truth grows into the vastness of everlastingness by turning the planet earth into the truth in expression, the good place God intended in the beginning."

I asked why all people don't recognize the divinity within them, why many people live hopeless lives. A Brother answered, "Even today there on earth come the cries of spirit-entities who are trapped in man/woman bodies. These entities cry out to be free, to find the peace of God, to express their truth. Because they take themselves to the human collective mind instead of the God-mind, they turn themselves inside out. They express in the physical only and forget the entire truth of the spirit that is rooted in the vastness of God. They creep when they might fly. They starve when they might feast. They become savage when they might become creative geniuses.

"The greatness of this God of ours cannot be told here. This word or that word will not hold the possibilities. The God of the greatness of the universe will not stay to be painted. God will not place His entity into an object nor a person. God has the wonderful strength, goodness, purity, the only positive force that generates itself by the simple touch of the God-mind."

But how, I wondered aloud, do human beings keep away the multitude of negative thoughts that pour into them from the collective human mind? How do we resist that which men and women have accepted as truth since the beginning of recorded history—and before? Just how do we touch this God-mind that has the answers to all our questions and that has the substance to fill all our needs?

"To become one with God you must empty your ego entirely. This empty ego will hold to the truth that God gives the only truth worth having, and the only truth that you want. The collective human mind then touches you no more than a fly who lights only to be shooed away. You must understand this truth concerning your ego, for only you can empty it. Your ego empties of its own will, not through force. There is never force. There is always free will.

"There are many who believe that God should step in and take over against the free will of the spirit-entities that inhabit the bodies. This principle—that people must have free will—cannot and will not be overridden, however. The reason for this principle is that there is no positive force, no goodness unless this goodness comes from willingness—the will that determines to do something. When a person has the willingness to have God express in his life—then a great explosion comes within that spirit. The explosion is the energy of God expressing. The good that comes explodes into being. This tremendous force we speak of is the natural consequence of the good expression that comes through the free will of individuals.

"God is there, but everyone has the CHOICE of accepting the great power or rejecting it. We in this Brotherhood have made our choices for this God of the Universe, this God of Truth. This CHOICE must be made by each individual, not by the God of the Universe. The individual has free will to create his own being, his own world to live in. This truth abides, and the open channel we provide takes the truth of God to you to use or not to use. This is our good message: Take the truth of God that you may prosper, that you may find your life easy, that your good will manifest, thus proving to you that God who loves you will be your teammate forever."

CHAPTER 11

CRYING IN THE WILDERNESS

*What is the difference between earth-mind and God-mind,
and how can I make the best use of both?*

"The earth-mind encompasses human thought from the beginning of time to the present. God-mind teams up with the God of the Universe to bring each person into contact with truth that is eternal. Therein lies the difference. This is not to say that earth-mind is all bad, for it holds basic truth that you refer to as common sense. And it is this common sense which helps you live successfully at the practical level of life."

Those in the Brotherhood warn, however, that earth-mind also contains a body of so-called truth that brings about most of mankind's troubles. They explain that this mind contains powerful thoughts that people think about, write about, and give their attention to. They point out that, unfortunately, much of this thought concerns negativity. Therefore, earth-mind produces fear, greed, suspicion, hate and revenge.

Since the earth-mind spills its contents on us continuously, I wondered how anyone can escape thoughts that create misery. In response to my concern, one Brother gave this piece of advice. "Announce to your individual mind that you are under the protection and guidance of the God of the Universe." That way erroneous earth-mind thoughts will be thrown away, according to this advanced spirit, and only common sense ideas that are of real help will be kept.

After my communicator signed in one morning by saying, "This is the Brotherhood of God here," the announcement came that information would begin about our world which cries for the God of our hopes, not the God of our negative thoughts. "People want to know this God of the Universe, the God that teams up with them and enters their lives. To reach the point of becoming one with God, there must be that pretentious hope that God is what He says He is—the pure and tender team that works on your behalf. Therefore, trust the truth that enters and teaches your being individually, *not the truth that people give to you.*

"People who teach the untruth that God brings famine or that God wreaks His vengeance upon people erode the power that is available to them, the God-power that will tone their bodies to health and touch their fields with harvest. Those who give their thoughts and words to this erroneous concept of God unite to bring about devastation. Thoughts, both positive and negative, turn into things; this is a principle of God. Therefore, famine, war, and conflicts manifest when they become powerful thoughts that team up with the substance of the universe."

People create the tone of life by their use of thought, according to those in the Brotherhood. Therefore, it is quite possible to invert the truth, and in that way empty out the power of God. A powerful thought of destruction may enter earth-mind where it continues to manifest, and the world is kept in turmoil. "This is why God, who has this power to use, cannot act. The only way to get the power of God to manifest is through the people who believe in and accept this power to do its work.

"As for the others, they see only the deepest despair. They manufacture the results of despair, and despair becomes reality.

"The truth of God is given here and there to try to punch holes in the onerous thought made concrete. The truth would wipe out this man-made concrete in hours if enough people would accept truth into their minds and into their hearts. Truth, simply put, means that God has provided the wonderful substance that creates all things. People have the power over this substance but do not use the power. They enter into the knowledge of the substance of the universe, but they do not see the connection between the way all material is composed and the power they have to create this material. Believers want more people to use the power because there is no limit; there is no certain amount of powerful substance allotted to each person. Take, take again, take still again. There is no end to what you can have here."

I cannot help contrasting this unlimited supply of God's substance with the earth-mind concept that there is just so much money and resources available, so it stands to reason some people must be poor. Therefore, when we accept only the truth of earth-mind, we cannot think of *plenty*. We think of *lack*. But when we accept the truth of God-mind, we think in terms of endless supply, a proliferation of substance that we use creatively.

People reach into earth-mind, according to those in the Brotherhood, to find the collective wisdom and the collective ignorance. Apparently many of us do not know the difference between what is wise and what is ignorant. However, they give us a way to become selective in what we accept as truth in the living of our lives.

"The thought that collects in the human or earth-mind makes its bed in the nothingness of the person who provides an empty place for it. Emptiness is the problem, you see. Emptiness sucks into it the thoughts that this human earth-mind collects, and it provides no way to sort out these thoughts. Emptiness merely needs to be filled with something—anything. If the truth of God was there, the thoughts that come from this collective mind would be sorted through. Then the ones that had value would remain, and the others would be blown away like chaff.

"The thoughts that filter through the human brain try to take root daily. There is only one way to turn the procedure into the creative venture it can be. That is, put the thoughts to the test of God. The test is simple. Tell the individual mind that the soul is under the truth of God. The mind will respond to this command. Then each must turn to the God he or she knows at whatever level the person knows Him.

"The God a person acknowledges will try these thoughts, accept those that pass the test of truth and take the others to be purified. That way the individual is protected from the ravages of erroneous thoughts. Also, in this way a person contributes to the teaching contained in the collective earth-mind. Here is how it works: God's energy turns erroneous thoughts into truth, and the person, in turn, teaches this new truth to the collective earth-mind.

"The energy that God has will turn the erroneous thoughts to the LIGHT. Then the collective earth-mind improves and grows in truth that gives the earth much hope. Each person may contribute to truth and to growth in God. Even persons who for some reason feel they can do little more than think, perhaps because their bodies will not work properly, can contribute to the collective earth-mind that will bring the good truth to the people."

One of the Brothers again discussed that part of the collective mind called common sense. "It is the mind that all have in common because it has been built up through the years to give mankind the intuitive thought that can give protection, physical help, and touch lives with practical earthly good." And again came the explanation that though earth-mind has a body of good common sense, it also has an abundance of "false truths, the so-called truth that passes for the right thing." Apparently the earth-mind reports whatever it is that people have come to believe.

"The message from earth-mind is frequently hopeless," my communicator states. "The hopelessness sometimes has to do with the teaching that men and women will inevitably destroy themselves. This truth is not of God-mind. It is of collective earth-mind. This so-called truth teaches that people head for their destruction because they wish to be destroyed. They think they have no choice. They get this untruth that we will not work for the cause of peace. To correct such an earth-mind truth, there must be the inner teaching of the difference between the God-mind and the earth-mind.

"The God that people speak of often is only the God that they build of their own reflection. They see hate, they see punishment, they see distrust. Therefore, it makes sense to them to believe that this God they build will destroy such people as they. This kind of untruth goes into the earth-mind where it resides and grows, for people give power to that which they think on in their hearts.

"Therefore, the earth-mind that contains the bits and pieces of both the truth and the untruth touches everyone the same. Untruth brings despair to many because it touches individuals with its outrageous message of hopelessness. The error-filled thoughts earth-mind accumulates give people much to worry about, for they produce fears, give inner pictures of the entire universe in uproar, and present the idea that their planet is doomed.

"The earth-mind rejects God-mind and teaches that there is no such thing as God-mind. The Brotherhood weighs the terrible troubles that people have, and they wonder why this earth-mind, which gives out the truth and untruth indiscriminately, has such power over people.

"Teaming up with people, you see, is that LIGHT which is the truth of God manifesting. This truth says that there is a wider view, a touch of God-mind that is superior to *either* the truth or untruth emptied by the earth-mind. It is the LIGHT making itself felt. It is the teaching of God manifesting through human beings that proves they can turn to God-mind only."

At this point one of the Brothers addressed the reader directly. "Take this idea into your mind now. Take this thought into the emptiness that cries out to be filled. The truth that God will fill each and every person who has needs is *true*. There is no need known to man that God-mind cannot take care of. This truth must be accepted to bring manifestation about. This truth—that God's power tries to get through so each person may manifest the thing or the condition that will meet the need—takes precedence over all others.

"The idea that men and women must give themselves to suffering, to heartache, to loneliness is false. Take this power. Turn toward the truth of God-mind that *there is this power*. Turn it into meeting your need. Do this now. No one should give himself or herself to the idea that there are situations that even God cannot meet." Again the message turns directly to the reader. "This false idea comes from earth-mind, not God-mind. Take the truth to heart here. Take the touch that God's love gives to you. Receive the good that this power will give. Don't think about whether you deserve it, or whether God thinks you are deserving. Think only of the power. Think of it working to meet the need or condition that turns the self to the truth."

The same Brother continued to address the reader. "This idea of the power is so important that we think we need to demonstrate it in some tantalizing way. Here is the promise. Take the truth into your mind, into your heart. Then unite with us to express your need or desire. Take this need or desire to the God that you understand best. Then enter it into the secret temple of your soul where God will refine it and beautify it so it will become even better than what you originally wanted. Then let go. Present the thing you receive to the world as that which God gives you. Tell others how this is done. Take the chance. Take the truth to work to your advantage. This great God of the Universe wants to give you good gifts. *Take!*"

I asked for examples from earth life with which people can identify. When people pray to be one with God and turn toward God-mind only for their truth, what can happen?

"There are some on the earth plane who pray that their situation be changed. When it is changed, they do not perceive this change as good. They say, 'Please, God. Take my life and make it work to the truth that You give me. Take my life over, God. Take my energy, my talent, my thoughts.' Then the life changes. When they put their lives into God's hands in this way, they sincerely want to make the change. But they do not really want the new interests or the new place or the new thoughts. They long for what was, rejecting this new good. They ally themselves with God to do wonderful things with their lives, but then they turn back because they fear the new situation."

One Brother used me as an example. "This writer wants to be one who gives her life to God, to His work. Then when this offer is made, she often wonders if this life will take too much of the past away. Are we right?"

Unfortunately, they were right. I asked if I would have better use of the power of God if I were more single minded toward this opportunity. "This power is for all regardless of their mind-set. However, there is greater response when the individual speaks with authority than when he pleads or speaks with a hesitant manner. There is no one who speaks to this power who is denied. But to those who give their truth, the empty place in their hearts, there is the explosive force that yields immediate response. This is the truth.

"There will always be those who speak of God with their mouths, but their hearts take the opposite view. Then their speaking becomes only empty words that take no power from the universe. They fall on the ground without becoming manifest. They wend their way into doubt, into the idea that God has denied the request. There must be an entering into the entire thought with the entire person—not just the word that gives the ear its touch. The ear will receive the word. The heart is referring to the God-self, to that spirit-entity that wants oneness with God. There is no teaming up with God unless a person takes his entire being to this truth.

"There will be the hopeless who will receive this power into their lives, but they will team up with it only to receive inspiration, not to manifest their needs. They seem satisfied with only the inspiration. They tell of this inspiration. They tell of their truth that gave them this wonderful feeling, this great magic touch. But they do not manifest.

"There will be some who call out, 'Help!' They cry out to God, 'Give me the energy I need to work, to live, to enjoy my life.' They cry out and they cry out. But they never get the entire thought together. What do they want? Healing? The teaming up with God? The teaming up with the Brotherhood to learn more truth? They simply take their cries into the wilderness of their empty thoughts, their empty desires, their empty needs. They think they need something, but they know not what. How can power fill the need or the condition that is desired unless that need or desire is expressed? Why will people just cry out—wail into the night or the day about their unhappiness without thinking through to what they need or desire to change their situation? They need goals. They need the thought clearly in mind. Then their cries can be acted upon.

"There are temples within people that hold that which is of value. These temples, these inner secret places, record the soul's deepest desires. Touching these inner temples with God-power is what is needed. These inner temples house that which is most precious to us, that which we probably would tell no one of. Telling the secrets of this temple would be sacrilegious."

One of the group then spoke directly to the reader. "Be true to the temple within you. Think of what you have put there. Take these things out during the time that you spend with God. Take these things out and tell God you wish to manifest these things. Then the power will spring forth to enter this temple, to take these things and put them into your own life experience. They will manifest because the powerful energy of God wants them to manifest. The attraction between that which is true within you and that which makes these things come true is irresistible. Take this message into the truth center of your being, into your own God-self to be acted upon.

"Nobody who wants the great power of God will be denied. This is the truth. That truth, however, is ignored, ridiculed, taught to be the foolishness that turns men into dreamers. That the reader may not heed the earth-mind advice on this subject, we recommend that the reader turn to the God of the Universe and tell Him that He is in charge now. There is no word except His. There is no power except His. There the God of the Universe will be—touching you with His power, with His truth. This is the truth we speak here."

One advanced spirit admitted that people can prosper in earth-life without God-mind, at least for part of their lives. "The idea that some people turn themselves into the opposite of what God is, is the fact we must face. That these persons seem to have power is undeniable. That these who cling to the untruths take their growth to the earth-mind is the fact we must understand. They turn themselves entirely to the earth-mind, to the thought that there is no God, no divinity, no everlasting life.

"Banding together with earth-mind, and away from God-mind, puts you into the energy that earth produces. This energy will take you far because today it has much real truth in it, but inevitably this energy runs out and leaves you empty. Those who employ this energy cannot figure out where their energy went. They think they are finished, and as they try to find this energy again, they wonder if they will ever again think creatively. The earth-energy runs strong in the beginning, and then it goes down the drain without any thought of returning."

Those in the Brotherhood explain that earth-mind is receptive to change. Therefore, they try to boost the quality of the earth-mind energy by giving it their best truth. They say that we, too, can contribute to this endeavor as we grow in God-mind truth. However, no matter how much better the earth-mind truth gets, it is still only a "temporary respite" that you and I can use for a number of years—well into our maturity. However, sooner or later, this particular energy will let us down.

The reason for this let-down, according to these advanced spirits, is that the earth-mind only gives us facts *as we perceive them*. This means that though we may succeed in a great way for awhile, the earth-mind will eventually let us down because it does not have the entire truth. It is limited even as we are limited. Earth-mind is not the source of all truth; it is merely the source of the truth mankind has discovered up to this point in history.

One Brother projected this thought concerning the writing of this book: "This writer teams up with us to write what the God of the Universe wants written. She had no thought of writing in this way, but the entity that entered into her body entered to write this book. Therefore, she is now teamed up with us to accomplish her mission. This writing will enter the earth to accomplish its goal of giving people the opportunity to evaluate the entire picture so they may choose what mind to enter into—earth's or God's. That is the entire purpose of this writing, actually.

"The Brotherhood wishes to be the one to wrest the wrong

thinking from the minds of mankind. We want to cancel out the effects of the thinking that earth-mind teaches. There is no thought that exists on the earth plane that opens the mind to greater possibilities than the truth taught by God, for this truth is individual. The God of the Universe opens the way to the greatness within each one by the true thoughts that come from God-mind.

"Tell the readers that the main point of all this is that they be the God-person that they are intended to be. That way they will find the best expression, the true gift that God has for each. In this way people will prosper to become the beings they wish to become. They should take this truth to their hearts now in order to fulfill their highest potential."

I pointed out that though those in the Brotherhood speak of groups of people, seldom have they written of a single individual. I asked for a few examples of people who used only the earth-mind to prosper them during their lifetimes. Also, I asked for examples of people who discovered the God-mind.

Thereupon I received individual examples that can enlighten us about earth-mind and God-mind. "There was a person who gave herself to the practice of entering completely into the earth-mind. She was a scholar who taught philosophy, and she was honored for her teaching. She prospered in her profession, and she became the author of books.

"Then the energy ran out. Her expression of her growth-plan needed the true energy of God in order to continue. The plan that she understood was merely the earth plan, not the God plan. Therefore, when she accomplished all that she set out to accomplish, inspired as she was by earth-mind, there simply was no more to do, no more to wonder about, no more to inspire her. The plan was complete. Therefore, when she lost interest in life, she took her own life to team up with the nothingness that she believed in beyond the earth life.

"This ended that life, but when the new life opened to her here, when she saw her truth in perspective, she was saddened. This new life showed her how she had touched the earth life with the inferior truth, with the truth that was not the true growth material. Then this entity became repentant. She wanted to return to take this new insight with her, to become the person who used the God-mind truth that would never be depleted.

"She went back, this time entering this earth life to the people with whom she had worked. She loved these people, believed they would help her. But they were steeped in the earth truth, the earth-mind. They who had been her own students had learned their lessons too well. They taught this child the ways they believed in. This person grew up to again believe in the totality of earth-mind. This time she made use of the earth-mind as she had done before. However, the idea came into her mind that this path seemed familiar, that it did not seem to fulfill her needs. This time she sought for more answers, more truth, and this time she found it. In so doing, this entity went against her parents' beliefs, against her own former beliefs. This time she disappointed those who had been her students because she took herself to the truth of God.

"There was another person who entered earth life to become one with God by giving himself to the God-mind. This entity, gentle to the point of being effeminate, took his truth from the mind of God. This lifetime brought the entity energy to enter into the great truth of being, the great truth of this universe. He studied the heavens and learned much knowledge about the tremendous galaxy that earth is part of.

"This wonderful person taught others about what he found. Though he did not have the manly prowess that people admired, though he had too much gentleness to suit most people, they accepted his wondrous teachings anyway. People went beyond his appearances to the central core of the truth he expressed through his work and through his own personality. There is nothing that cannot be done with this tremendous truth that God takes to our minds when we reach out for it."

The word *truth* is used with both earth-mind and with God-mind, which some may find confusing. However, these advanced spirits explain that anything we believe in is our truth. Earth-mind holds "temporary truth" that serves us for the short term; however, "lasting truth" comes from God-mind and will take us the entire distance through our lifetimes.

Another explanation from an advanced spirit says that temporary truth can result in fame and fortune, but not in eventual satisfaction within our inner selves. Temporary truth will help us to manifest our goals, but when the goal is reached, we will believe there is nothing more to be attained. "Lasting truth," however, will lead us past our first goals to even greater accomplishments and deep fulfillment.

Those in the Brotherhood indicate that people on the earth plane who are blind to God-mind truth will be in great distress when they go to the next plane of life. "They know not who they are," one Brother stated. "They see flesh and blood, and they think that is all there is to them." This Christ-inspired group of spirits has the perspective to view the situation much more clearly than those of us who live in this earth plane. They say that those entities who come to this plane without a plan get a lot of their attention. These helpers see that those who do not understand their spiritual natures use the earth-mind truth to get their own ways and to get out of trouble by any means possible no matter whom they hurt.

"There is no truth they will accept but that which is the lowest form of earth-mind. These empty ones generate their own truth and thereby destroy themselves and others. These private truths, that give them no real and lasting good, only temporarily touch them with riches or with pleasure in the sensual realm."

When those who give themselves to unworthy truth get together, their grossness evolves into a terrible reality for everyone in the earth plane, one Brother asserts. "This grossness takes the form of hatred of all that is unusual, or productive or beautiful. And this coarseness tends its truth with zealousness and because it generates more of the same truth, it gives a pattern of violence and hatred in action. These who give themselves to hatred often take their troubles into their minds and focus on the people that supposedly cause these troubles.

"Taking this (so-called) truth of theirs into their depravity twists it into ugliness, but it still is their own truth. They must live with it. Unfortunately, the others in earth life must live with it, too. This unworthy truth they believe in goes into earth-mind. Thus this mind is filled with the negativity that thwarts good people, that presents the distortions, that provides the awful answers that people seek. This truth they twist and inject with their own energy so that it enters the minds and plays upon people's imaginations, gives them terrible thoughts to ponder, generates the force that destroys the true word. That picture is the evil side of things. But there is, of course, the other side.

"No one belongs to earth-mind. There is free will. The people who enter into this evil truth generate their own power, but they try to force their truth upon others. The act of forcing takes strength away from them, and their evil weakens. The truth that force is not strength or power is the inviolate principle we must pay attention to. Therefore, the power of God is in the willingness, not the forcefulness of God-mind entering into the entities who open their minds. Therefore, the evil that people think into existence loses its strength as it turns itself into the forcefulness that enters others to *make* them believe and act in evil patterns.

"Touching earth-mind takes no particular effort, for it hovers over you constantly. It gives its truth freely because it pours out into the emptiness that people have. The earth-mind truth empties itself into the vacuum that takes whatever is available. Taking from God-mind, however, requires a decision to do so. God-mind takes its truth from God only, and it gives on demand, on request, on the willingness to accept it. Then, and then only, it pours into a person's soul."

The difference between these minds, therefore, is quite clear. Thoughts from earth-mind pour endlessly upon us, whether we want them or not. They are like the rain that falls on the just and the unjust. However, when we give God the control, the right of way into our minds, only the useful earth-mind truth penetrates our minds along with the complete truth of God.

I asked for someone from the Brotherhood to comment on prosperity as being of God or of earth-mind, and here is how it is explained. "The truth of prosperity is that God gives the substance, the means by which people prosper. That is the easy way, the faith-filled way. But earth-mind teaches prosperity too. It says you, too, can 'get ahead' of others. You can be rich when others are poor. The earth-mind teaches that there must be poverty, that there is only so much prosperity to go around, and this prosperity takes the form of wealth. Then people get the earth truth that being the greatest, the most powerful, the best at anything is the way to prosper. There is no other way, according to earth-mind. That is, there is no other way unless you get prosperity by taking what you want by dishonest means.

"That people accept this false truth of earth-mind that says there are limitations is the wonder. This earth-mind insists that there is only the limited amount of prosperity, and if you are going to get yours, you'd better hustle all the time. Teaming up with the Brotherhood will help people manifest prosperity without all this hustle, without getting into false concepts, without giving the lie to their lives that their prosperity depends on their own cleverness, their own work, their own begging."

Many people reach identity crises in their lives. I asked how they might be affected by earth-mind. "That people may go for years somewhat happily immersed in the earth-mind truth is the way it is. These people depend on material things to satisfy them. They teach the untruth to themselves that this is all there is to life—the accumulation of fine things, the good life. But eventually the earth-mind truth no longer satisfies. Then people try to find meaning in their lives. But without God-mind, there is no meaning.

"They are spirit. That is their reality. Therefore, material things only satisfy the material in them. The greater part of them is the spirit, that which is of God, that which is indestructible, that which touches the God of the Universe. With this spark of divinity within them, they eventually must touch that which is divine. Either that or they eat themselves up in their worries, their troubles, their promises that their lives will be the best. People promise themselves the good life, but when they attain it, they then touch the emptiness within. Earth-mind truth no longer fills them, no longer pleases them, for it is not the reality which they are."

CHAPTER 12

PROGRESSING SPIRITS—STORIES ABOUT THE BROTHERHOOD

How did you, the Brotherhood, grow into advanced souls?

People who seriously consider reincarnation as God's plan for their soul growth inevitably want to know the specifics—names, dates, places of past lives. They want to know exact accomplishments and titles, if any. I asked someone in the Brotherhood to comment.

"The specifics, as you call them, tell us nothing of soul growth. They only tell of the earth life lived in one tiny period. This lifetime becomes insignificant after you see the entire spectrum of lives, you see. The growth is what matters—not the specific lifetime which may have yielded so little in the way of success. The history of lifetimes, in fact, becomes boring to recite. This exactness you mention gives us no insights, no responsible touching of the truth of our being.

"One lifetime—what is that? This one lifetime that you think is so much is, in fact, so tiny in time that the measure is hardly worth taking. That the truth was held onto, that is important. That the truth was demonstrated in whatever way the plan provided for, that is the important record. The growth of the soul—that steady progress toward the truth, toward the God of the Universe, there is the meaty part of the story!"

These advanced spirits offer several stories from their own group—stories that show their failures, their progression, their growth. Each story told gives the reader a unique perspective into the purpose of reincarnation. "The goal," one Brother said, "is that others may understand that this method we give is their method, too. The reader takes the proof of our overcoming to his heart to enact that same kind of overcoming for himself.

"Here is the first story about a Brother who became the truth in expression. He came to the earth life to be the pure undaunted entity that the God of the Universe wanted to have. He gave himself to the people to be their entree to the God of the Universe whom he called the Father. This Brother led others because his truth was irresistible. His truth gave them hope to the better way of the great brotherhood that God wanted. The people went to him to get their healing, their hopes fulfilled, their true selves touched with his spirituality. They gave him their honor and their good thought.

"Then people pressed him to do even more. They wanted him to lead them from the bondage of the oppressor. But this Brother would not do this because his mission was not to have earthly power, but to have spiritual power. To understand this truth, the people finally had to see him crucified and dead and then resurrected. Then they knew the spiritual power was real, and it gave them great joy and happiness. This resurrection, this rebirth of the body itself, gave these people hope that became real. The hope was vague at first, but the real body was the material that convinced them.

"They went here and there to spread the truth that this Brother brought to them. "They taught the truth, the light, the Fatherhood of God. Then they created a religion that they named after the hope they once had of the Christ that would come to deliver them. They called this new religion Christianity. This religion was the one that incorporated the Jewish religion but went on to incorporate the risen entity named Jesus the Christ.

"Growth took place in abundance for a long while. People grew to love the one named Jesus even if they did not see him. They gave him their loyalty, their devotion. Finally they made him God, and they lost the entire meaning of his entry into their midst.

"This Brother came to this plane determined to widen the scope of this Counselor, this Brotherhood, so that his truth would not be lost. That people would take this Counselor to their hearts and to their minds was his hope. He is even now giving us many assignments that will change earth life from the pursuance of the half-truth to the complete truth. This Brother has no thought except to further the truth of God within individuals. For this he works with us here on this plane even though he can go on past this plane to other planes. His is the perfect alignment with the God of the Universe, the true One-with-God.

"No one can ever be more than Jesus was on earth. He gave the perfect pattern. That he is the only one who can have this true alignment is simply not true, however. He came that others may take him at his word that what he did others can do and even more. Jesus teamed up with the Brotherhood to accomplish his own destiny as the son of God who taught others that they too are sons and daughters of God.

"This perfection he attained puts many off because they think they can never be perfect. But they do not understand what perfection is. They think perfection is soft-spoken, that it is a trusting face, brotherly action or great belovedness that emanates from the face. They believe that everyone is drawn to that perfection, and that there is a halo to identify it. Surely, they think, perfection is the temple that has no flaw. *But this is not the truth at all.*

"Perfection is of the inner God-self where the mind of God feeds the soul. This person, this entity, this being that shows forth perfection takes no thought for pleasing men and women. This perfection pleases God only, pleases the total goodness that gives itself to this being. There is no perfection that pleases men and women the whole time, you see. People will question goodness as the selfish thought, the thought that may cause strife, the thought that is not in the Bible or some such questioning. This questioning is the thing to ignore within oneself.

"The Brother of whom we speak ignored the thoughts that

sought to get him away from the God-self that knew the truth. He ignored the questions by giving them simple answers and going on his way. There is no way to avoid the questions, but one can avoid giving them thought-focus. The wonderful truth within us will be the guide, the most reliable helper and comforter. The truth within is the only one to pay attention to, not the truths of others. This Brother was perfect within himself. He gave himself to the God of his being, the God of the Universe, the God whose goodness surpasses the best concept of man."

The Brotherhood began with the supreme example—Jesus the Christ—because his is the ultimate example. They explain how he attained his oneness with God by living his earth-life plan exactly as he and God worked it out. Next, they tied Jesus' attainment into our own potential for similar perfection. Jesus is, as they said in an earlier chapter, "the Brother of Brothers," but Jesus is not pictured as aloof, vaporous perfection. They present him as the reality, the advanced spirit that each of us is trying to be. However, most of us will identify with stories of other spirit entities—stories that chronicle failures as well as successes.

"The next Brother we speak of," my communicator continued, "began his being in the universe as the spark of divinity that had the perfect freedom that we spoke of in the last chapter. This entity devoted his divine spark to the plan to be one who would give himself to our Brotherhood/Counselor to help him in his earth life. He tried to be a paragon (of perfection), but the open channel he thought to create became clogged with his ego. He had no God to emulate, no God to worship.

"He made a great monument to the God he worshiped, but he forgot the truth he came to teach because he worked on the monument. This monument became the great pyramid in Egypt. This pyramid became his monument to the God he knew, but he forgot the truth he came to tell to others.

"Then in his death and his new life here, he gave himself to the study of his previous lifetime. He saw this monument as a thing the earth did not need. He had caused misery in the building of it and had taught people nothing of the truth he had planned to tell. Eventually he returned to earth life again, this time even more determined to tell people about the truth of God. This time he again became immersed in the monument idea, and he built still another memorial, another tomb that his body rested in. There it stood, the pyramid again. This time the pyramid was not in Egypt but in another land across the world.

"Then he came to earth life to try again to tell the truth to people. This time he opened himself to the Counselor/Brotherhood, and the temple of truth within him poured forth his truth to people everywhere. The monument idea was changed to truth which he poured forth into the great ideas that invaded countries as the message of God. This message developed as he turned his mind to us, to his help, to his teachers. This message taught that God gives the truth. The truth is not of man's own observation. The truth is growth from God, not the approval of the truth of people. The message he brought gave people a new hope of the spirit that inhabited their bodies, the spirit that had given its attention to the truth of men instead of the truth of God. This new truth, that they were to look for within themselves, gave these people new control over their lives, new tenants to old bodies.

"The third Brother we will tell of planned to be the messenger that God wanted to speak to people about the truth of their beings. But in his earth life, his mind went instead to his selfish desire to be the only person who could manifest truth to the people. This egotistic expression of God gave people some hope, but not much. They looked to this Brother for their help, but did not look within themselves. Instead of telling them the truth, he held the truth for himself only. He kept others in darkness, and thereby missed the mark he came for.

"When he came to earth life again, he came to please the God-self that proclaimed the truth of God to all people. This time he did this teaching, but he wandered too far into the wide spaces of the mind so that people thought he must be crazy. They gave him little heed, gave him little attention except to think him the man who tried to be the God of the weird ones. This Brother, in contemplating his life when he reached the next plane, wanted to try this same plan again.

"He returned to earth life yet another time to give his message. This time he came without ego, without his own selfishness. He came to serve, and serve he did. This time he brought the message of God into the quiet places of the earth—the rural places, the small villages. He wandered here and there giving out the truth, and he had no thought for his own needs except to manifest his supply as he needed it. His spirituality grew within him, and he even progressed to the point where he could make his body come and go from plane to plane and thus move his body to distant places. This soul, this Brother, was the true guru who wandered in the vastness of India.

"The fourth Brother came to understand the needs of those who cried out in sickness. The sickness that this soul wanted to minister to was the kind that kept the individual from becoming the true child of society. This disease was the one that gave people scars, gave them the fear of death. The disease left them without strength, without the force of good life. The Brother became the physician to help these people, to help them with this illness, this infirmity. Teaching people how to care for themselves, he tried to lead them to the expression of their wholeness. This he did and continued to do throughout his lifetime without regard to his own gain or desire.

"When the spirit of this one came to this plane to contemplate his life, he thought of his life on earth, thought of how he helped those with this disease. Then he realized his mission must be to go again to teach people not only how to attain healing without the help of a physician, but to continue in health without the help of a physician. He went again into the earth plane to express his plan. This time he took his concern to the ministry of the truth that the body responds to the mind. This mind, of course, is the mind that captures the thought of all mankind into what is known as the collective earth-mind truth. This earth-mind truth gives people the truth that they observe, but it does not give them the inner spiritual truth. This earth-mind truth brought people the idea that all disease is a great possibility.

"The Brother tried to change that earth-mind concept of illness. But he could not do this. He tried but he could not change it. Then he gave himself to teaching the spiritual healing that the Brothers gave him to be his tool. He used this tool, but he could not get others to use it. They looked to him as 'The Healer,' but they would not accept these powers of healing for themselves. He tried to give the truth, but he could not. But he did carry out his purpose, and for that he grew spiritually into the advanced soul who could work successfully in the Brotherhood.

"When we say Brother we mean the feminine person also. But the translation we use here usually takes the masculine form to be more convenient. This next Brother was a woman in the earth life that gave her the opportunity to become the advanced person who now works within the Brotherhood. This woman spirit-entity gave her life to the truth that worked with the growth of the God spirit in bodies with undeveloped brains.

"She worked to develop teamwork between the mind of God and the mind of the human body. These people always thought as children; they could not bring their brains to express mature thoughts, mature truth. But when she worked with these people, she taught them that their brains, which would not serve them well, gave them enough power to understand that they were spirit-entities who had the divine spark. This spark, she taught them, could be nourished if they would turn within to it.

"These thought-expressions, these entities in underdeveloped brains, gave themselves over to the truth within themselves, and they grew spiritually in that lifetime. The Brother kept on the thought that they were divine sparks of God himself. These thought-entities began to grow, to manifest spiritually, and some began to manifest on the material level, enlarging their capacity to use their brains. She gave herself to her work tirelessly, and she gave the truth without fear of the opinions of others.

"She also gave her truth without the fear of what others preached to her, that what she taught would ruin her. She gave her word to these undeveloped brains, and those who would receive it made great strides in their own growth. Those who live with undeveloped brains team up with God easily. They enter into the wonderful truth without question. Teaming up with this truth teaches them how to enter into God's own teamwork, and they grow in the open way that true believers grow.

"The next Brother entered earth life by way of the body of an adult. She solved the problems and touched the lives of those who were affected by the first soul's inability to come to terms with the troubles she found. This soul, this second possessor of this body, straightened out the affairs of that person before she worked on the plan she brought to earth life.

"This new soul took her truth to those who had no plan within them, the ones who returned to earth too hastily without thinking through a new plan. This Brother ministered to those who remained empty until truth entered their minds to form a plan to carry them to their goal of growing spiritually in this lifetime.

"This Brother took her truth to those she found within the prison walls, to those she found in desolate places without hope for the next day. These were the ones she taught the truth of their beings—that they were spirit-entities who had the divine spark of God within them. Their hopeless condition indicated they had lost their awareness of this truth, for those who knew their true greatness that brought them into oneness with God found success in life and living. Teaming up with the Brotherhood, she taught with authority, taught with the energy that God gives on request. This teaching of hers became the generous premise that those without hope can be reached with the truth.

"Among these advanced spirits are many who began their existence thinking that they were gods themselves. These Brothers wandered into the earth to experiment with the life forms and became those who were trapped there. Then when they developed true understanding, they became the advanced souls. This understanding came only after many lifetimes. These who came into the earth and became trapped in materiality gave themselves the falsehood that they were the only good, that what they experienced was the real good, that their wandering into the earth to live in the forms there amounted to greatness. This ego took them to their entrapment, to their misled notions, to their getting of new truth—earth truth—

which made life hard.

"But the Brothers who began in this way have learned the errors of that way of thinking, and they lived many lifetimes to grow and mature into advanced souls. The stories we tell here give some notion of how souls mature, how they work through their truth to the understanding of oneness with God being the only truth to give their attention to.

"The next Brother we will tell of exists in this plane now as an individual who gives his energy to develop the thought that each person has something special to give to the earth life. He teams up with God to give the gifts which, in turn, help each spirit express his growth plan.

"This spirit entity came to earth many times to make his growth what it is today. The Brother came both as a man and as a woman and used his talents finally to express the energy of God in Beauty. This one has the ability now to encourage the expression of talents—all talents. He energizes these talents when asked to do so, when the soul wishes that help. Then he enters the mind of the person to give what earth people call 'inspiration.' This inspiration takes the person to new heights of expression. The Brother brings the person to the inner knowledge of the God of the Universe who withholds nothing that the person may ask for in the name of God's goodness. This is true what we tell here.

"Being the truth-peddlers who enter earth life to help people express their true selves, we believe we need more work, more people to call upon us. God gives us this special task, this task of helping in all ways to join the earth lives with the God-life. But we need more to do, more spirits to counsel, more truth-hungry persons to help." The communicator then appealed directly to the reader. "Be the ones to give yourselves to this help. This help is better than riches, better than any singular earthly material goal. This help will achieve even more than one or two earthly goals. The earthly goals take on insignificance compared with the truth that God will provide the energy to manifest ALL things that are good."

I often refer to the Brotherhood as "they." It seems to me—a feeling mostly—that I am working with a group of spirits. I asked for a comment. "The Brotherhood is made up of many spirits, but there is one especially who is working with you. This spirit is the one who leads you along to receive these messages, who helps you to tune in to this truth." I asked if this particular spirit has a name. There was a hesitation before the response came. It seems the name of this Brother has to do with his character and is not translatable. Later, I decided that a name might put us on a very personal level, and it's obvious to me that these teachers/counselors want me to center on God-mind, not a particular personality.

However, I asked if the Brother working with me had given his own story here, and this is what came. "This story has the same terms that the others have. The story began when I was one with God living in total freedom. That I entered the earth life is the truth. That I became one of those who was trapped is true, too. That I lived lifetime after lifetime to express the truth is also true. That I grew in spirit is true also. That I grew into the advanced soul finally is true also. This is my own truth that I give here, but it is not the entire picture. The truth that I give has only the elements. This truth is the truth that I brought into being. Truth that one brings into being is the kind that will become part of oneself."

I was somewhat disappointed. I had hoped for more insight into this spirit with whom I work day after day. Later in the day a story came through, a story told in third person, a story that apparently came with some reluctance.

"The Brotherhood wants me to tell you of still another Brother. This one has the elements of the three greatest souls who ever manifested on earth. This soul made the trip to earth life again and again, but he did not get the greatness of the plan executed. Then when this soul finally took the concept of the great power of the truth with him, the lifetime yielded the greatness he wanted to express. This soul took the truth he knew, applied it to his plan, turned the situation into the manifestation of the goodness that is of God. Then this soul, satisfied with his plan in execution, took our tests here and passed with flying colors.

"This soul opens his heart to those who enter life to become one of the specialists, the ones who specialize in some aspect of truth—such as this writing. This soul wants the specialists who enter this communication to become true receivers, not just authorities who can contact this plane. The truth aspect is his true vocation here. This spirit is myself, the one with whom you communicate. This spirit is the entree of the ones in earth life who want to enter into correspondence with this plane in order to grow. This was your own cry, the need for a teacher," my messenger said to me. "This teacher is our person, our spirit self—the one with whom you communicate here."

Like anyone else, I am often filled with anxious thoughts for people I care about. During the writing of this chapter, these words came to encourage me: "The Brother to whom you communicate knows it is not always easy to empty your mind to receive this material, but he wants you to know that this work is the truth that is coming through you. Think on this truth as that which gives the best that there is to others. Then you will know the true goodness expressing through you. Think not for the worries in your life or in the lives of others. Bless the situations, empty your mind of worry or concern. Think only to give the worry to us, for we will carry it to encourage your work here. Take no thought for any worry that comes to mind, for there is nothing that can overcome our truth, our good that expresses within you, within Carl"—my husband—"within that which concerns you."

With this overwhelming assurance, we continued with the writing of this chapter. "Some souls tell us they grow to be one of us, but indeed they do not. Some want to help, want to be part of this group of helpers, but they do not have the qualifications they need. This understanding is the essence of the Brotherhood—that the God of the Universe takes the true open personifications of truth to be one of us. The others who apply may try, but they enter our group only to fall away because their understanding is an inferior one. Only the illustrious, the advanced souls, take the work and get it done here.

"There must be advanced understanding of truth, advanced understanding of contact, advanced understanding of the power that truth has to give. The Brotherhood opens itself to each person, each entity, but only those who can pass the great tests can work with the ones in the earth plane. The others turn aside in the lack of understanding and the lack of skill. They may elect to try again; that is, to go back to earth life to work out more growth. Then they may come back to us to try again to pass the great truth tests.

"The next Brother we will tell about united with the God of his disbelief. Then he went into the marketplace where he touched others with his beliefs that brought others into his unholy activities. He entered into the unholiness of taking people's lives as the judge over others. He sought to play the God of life and death for others. His greatest regret is that he taught others his untruth, and that he led others into the way of disbelief in the truth of God. These two betrayals came about because he listened to earth-mind instead of God-mind.

"But when he went to this plane, he saw and understood the open channel's truth that gave him insight into his great betrayals. Then he re-entered life on earth to become the opposite of what he had been before. This Brother gave himself to teaching the truth of God to others, enlarging their concepts of the truth that they are God's true spirits, God's best entities. This one awakened the divine spark in many. He turned himself into the open channel for truth. He undertook nothing that was not for good. He became the one to offer himself to be the recompense to others who might try to condemn the truth. He went to the end of his life as the truth-teller regardless of the punishment he received, regardless of the hurt he received. He remained loyal. Then when he re-entered this plane, he had turned his God-self into the advanced soul who could join the Brotherhood to give the help that people need. This growth is indeed possible if a person remains the truth personified, the truth in action.

"The Brotherhood is made up of these souls who wound their way back to the God of the Universe. These souls went out again and again to take their truth with them. Sometimes they failed, sometimes they half won, sometimes they completed their tasks and no longer had to return to earth unless they entered life again in the adult body to do some special task. No wonder the truth enters the earth life slowly. This lifetime after lifetime is the slow way. That we—the souls who lost their way—have returned to God as well as we have is the wonder."

CHAPTER 13

RECEIVING THE TRUTH FROM GOD-MIND

How do you explain this communication between us?

In the second chapter, "Forming a Partnership," I gave my own story about this communication with the Brotherhood of God. In this chapter, my communicator gives the explanation of how this writing/reception works.

"This truth we give about our communication will be our truth, not yours," they told me. "You will not understand how all this can be real, but do not worry, for we give the truth as always. We have our view of this communication which must be added to yours, you see, for we give the way this thought transference really happens, not the way it seems to happen. Now tune us in to the spirit entity that you are. Tune out the physical part."

I focused on the plow into the soft earth. I was as ready to receive as I had ever been, but nothing came. I waited—nothing. Then came "Nb Nnnnn ? Nv; NgNnnnnnnnnn." What was wrong? I waited.

"The wetness that we feel here is because the truth is the part that gives the impetus to the whole communication," the Brother stated. "This being (Jean K. Foster) who writes to you will not invigorate the communication at all."

The Brotherhood uses unique but appropriate vocabulary to describe situations. There was indeed a "wetness" on the communication. And though I tried to connect to that truth, I could not do this from my own energy.

"That which invigorates this message is God-mind itself. Unless a person tunes in to this Mind, there is a lack of understanding." And they proved this fact when they withdrew the open channel to God-mind. They explained that they tried to further the communication by just our beings touching. However, there is no way to receive this great truth except through the God-mind connection.

I asked if the Brothers and I talk person to person just as two people in the earth plane talk to one another. "Are we," I asked, "just two entities who share our truth?"

"That is the way it is. The truth we have here may be for your own good, but the truth that we bring through this open channel from God-mind is the *absolute* truth. None of us is able to hold this truth alone or even collectively. This truth is held only by God. Be the one to use this open channel, and you touch this gold mine of truth."

To receive this God-mind truth, these advanced spirits say that you and I must do three things: First, acknowledge the God-mind principle. This means we must take this concept to our inner self where the God of the Universe will reach us with truth that we will understand.

Second, we must give time to the work of this communication. It is not a first-time thing. There must be practice, and there must be openness. Also, we must use the power of God to make this work.

And third, the thing that finalizes this communication is our acceptance of the reality of the next plane of life. "You must have a realization that this plane of life, which is invisible to those on the earth plane, is real. This plane of life belongs to the truth that life continues past what you call death. That is the final part."

There are, of course, various considerations to take into account in becoming a good communicator with the Brotherhood of God and thereby God-mind. "There is the matter, too, of becoming the kind of person who can meet life on your own terms. If you must meet life on the terms of other people, this writing will not prosper." It is necessary, the explanation states, that there be confidence between the source of truth, God-mind, and your inner being. If you and I must check out the opinion of other people before we consider the message real truth, we won't receive a clear message.

There is another matter which those in the Brotherhood rate as very important to good communication, and that is our understanding of thought. "Thought is combined with substance. It is real, it is vital, and it is open to your suggestion."

Another point they mention is to understand our true nature which is spirit, not flesh. Therefore, they say, "It is natural to the person who accepts this point of view to communicate with other entities who are spirit. This matter of the spirit being the reality and the body being the temporary good must bring forth the acceptance of this communication. Planning to become a pontificator takes its resoluteness from our acceptance of the truth that we each exist."

It seems easy, this business of communication, but it isn't. "This communication must be your thought which is adjusted to our thought and then funneled through God-mind. We must position our thoughts into the proper wave lengths, the proper fields of contact. This contact is our work here.

"The truth or proof of our touch is this book. This thought transference from us to the writer to the paper by way of this typewriter gives us much pleasure. We have learned much about how this entity (Jean) thinks." I winced, for I still am not used to the complete openness of communicating with our thoughts. "This entity often tries to bring in her own beliefs, but we give her a nudge of sorts. We take our message away, and there she is with nothing to say. Then she realizes that she is writing on her own. At this point she backs up and crosses out the material that she can see is her own.

"This teacher-student relationship takes the place of the possible touching of God-mind she could do on her own if she could. If she were able, she would copy this writing that we give her by simply seeing the words in her mind. But she does not see them, so we give them to her through her God-self. There is no way to lead this writer astray by this writing. She is zeroed in on the true wave length that gives her access to God-mind. There is nothing to fear, for no evil lurks within God-mind.

"The evil that entities fear when they give themselves to this writing are those spirits that they accept as sources of truth simply because they are on this second plane of life. There is no particular wisdom about being in this second plane of life. We all go here." According to this Brother, if we write and listen only to those spirit entities on the next plane of life, we do not grow. The reason we do not learn great truth is that "many here may know even less than those in the earth plane."

Though we may wish to contact someone dear to us who has gone to the next plane, that person is not the source of our absolute truth. "The open channel formed by the Brotherhood/ Counselor is the only outer contact on this plane that can help one make the God-mind contact," the Brother states. "However, there are others here who can be of much help to those on the earth plane. These will bring truth too, not the truth of God-mind, but the truth they have discovered for themselves. These entities want to help those in the earth plane because of some earth tie, some relationship or touch of love. These persons will come to those who request them." The spirit entities that we want to hear from will give us good advice, according to this advanced spirit. They will urge us to go to God for our truth, and they also give their truth when called on. But they must not stay indefinitely, for they must get on with their lives.

"You see, they take the place of the truth of God-mind, and that will not do for long. They merely take the truth they know and help people in the earth plane to become the ones to turn to God for answers. They try to warn them of wrong thinking, wrong acts and wrong decisions. They touch lives for good, but they must not stay long. These spirit entities must go on to their own truth, to their own living, their own work. They must continue to grow, you see, not just be nursemaids to those on the earth plane.

"This open channel's work entails bringing the truth that comes from God-mind to the entities who call for it. The Brotherhood holds the key, so to speak, to the truth that will set people free of their being's untruth. These spirits give themselves to the task of this work in the earth plane.

"The Brotherhood works now in the writer to bring this material. She does not have the entity's truth entirely in her being. She teaches what she knows, what she experiences, what she sees in the world and feels within her. These are the things she has written about in articles. But she has not been able to write the truth that appears here because she has not known of it. The only way this comes about is through the entity's open mind that is open to this channel where God-mind truth pours through. Then this entity writes it all down.

"The entity at times directs the writing by asking questions. The writing then gives itself to answers and explanations. The Brotherhood wrote the plan for the book, the outline, the truth of the book. There is no way for this entity to eliminate our help. There is no way as yet she can alone contact this God-mind. This entity knows this, for at the beginning of this chapter, we closed the channel, took ourselves out of the picture. There was nothing that made sense—only unrelated letters and unrelated words. That's what this book would be without our open channel that gives her the way to tune in on this God-mind. (In the future) she may enter an advanced state where she can make this contact on her own. Then she will form the open channel herself and be one with God.

"There is no way to begin this project that we have here unless the individual initiates it from the earth plane. Nobody will be open unless the person thinks contact is possible. Then the willingness gives power to the project. The entity who writes this book gave her energy to this project even though many times she was embarrassed to let anyone else know what she was doing. She gave this project time each day. She thought that we on this side were real, that we had a plan to lay before her, that we would be true to our word of helping her in all her personal problems as well as in the writing of this book.

"Many times we came together to work out the problems that closed the channel between the entity and us. These problems, unless resolved, tend to block the open channel because they seem all important in the individual's life. But problems respond to the enlightenment from God-mind, and people are freed from their earthly worries.

"Teaching this person to write in this manner was similar to teaching anyone to write who has not done so before. The touch of her hands on the pencil was the beginning. The touch on her typewriter was the second. Maybe one day we will speak face to face if she ever learns to tune in to us to see us with her earthly eyes. This is possible, but she has not done this yet.

"There is the matter of communicating from mind to mind. We get the writer's attention first, and we discuss whatever there is on her or our agenda. Then we proceed to the truth that comes from God-mind. That's the way it works—a progression. To become prolific in this writing, one must take the words that come without trying to make sense out of them at the moment. Take the mind to a far place to let this open channel function. We gave this writer the picture to focus on. We said to visualize the soft earth, and then the plow that cuts through the earth. 'The earth,' we told her, 'is you. The plow is this Brotherhood. This is the way you will write when we come together—by concentrating on that visualization, that picture in your mind that shuts out all other thought.' Because this worked effectively, we began to communicate.

"Later there were other obstacles. The writer objected to some of the truths she received. She gave her objections to us by thought and by stopping the writing in great consternation. The writer brought her own versions of truth with her, you see. The truth that we brought to her was new, and it was outrageous when compared to that which she was taught in life. The individual mind wanted to reject it, to correct it, to make it conform. She clung to her old truth rather than accept the truth from the Brotherhood's understanding and from God-mind because she had not as yet fully teamed up with us.

"There was no way for awhile to let the writer try the real truth, so we had to begin by counseling her on the personal level. Then she trusted us, you see. She saw that we were only interested in helping her, not leading her astray. Because the writer stayed with us, she gave her truth to us to reach into her mind to improve. Then she turned herself over to God-mind to improve. Finally, she turned herself over to God-mind entirely to receive the wonderful truth that will touch everyone with good.

"There is the truth that God brings. There is the truth that each person thinks he has for himself. The truth of individuals is both the real truth and the half-truth of earth-mind. But this being turned to us for God-mind because she wanted to give herself to this project, to the work of writing this book. When we first told her of the book plan, she reacted with shock. She told us she could not do it, that she was not qualified, that she had no background, but we had to override these thoughts.

"Therefore, the touch that we gave her was encouragement, hopefulness that this book would come into being. But this message was resisted for a long time—or so it seemed. This entity thinks the resistance was of short duration. But there is no way to explain our joy here when she finally capitulated to our requests and let herself be used for this important work."

At this point in our relationship, I was sure that no one knew me better than those in the Brotherhood. After all, they heard my thoughts. I turned more and more to them for counsel and guidance. "She began thinking we were the source of truth," they wrote. "But we had to teach her otherwise. She believed that we entered her mind as the ones with the truth, and she responded in that way. But finally we got across to her that we are the means, but we are not God-mind.

"This Mind takes its truth from the God of the Universe, the God unlimited, the God undeterred from the goals of absolute good. This idea that we gave the truth to her caused her to write amiss for awhile. Then we told her, gently, that the central idea was that God gave the truth, not we and not she. There is no ego here. Egos turn aside when truth pours through."

I remember that day and the words that made it clear to me that God is the source. I reacted with shock, as I remember. Perhaps I had begun to equate the Brotherhood with God. At any rate, their gentle nudge pushed me in the right direction, though I was somewhat chagrined at my error.

"There is no thought that enters this writer's mind in the state of her truth-getting which does not come from God-mind," the Brotherhood insists. Of course in my day-by-day living I contend with many thoughts that no doubt come from earth-mind. "The truth has its entire focus on becoming that which will enlighten people who read it. We have this book in our mind, and gentle thoughts of her best work guide her through it. Gentle thoughts that give her our commendation take her out of the understanding of her own work to the entity which touches God-mind. This thought persists that we and this writer tender our mutual thought toward the accomplishment of this task. To attain this objective, we give her suggestions on her work—when to work, how to enter her own questions, and even advice on getting a word processor to make the work go more smoothly and quickly.

"The thing that helped this writing to become the truth in expression is the writer's temerity—her boldness that challenged the words. She encouraged us to give further explanation that she might understand perfectly and that the reader could understand too. The book is richer because of this procedure.

"The writer takes her own feelings into this thought transference, but she does not empty these feelings into the book. There are times when she plans the writing so as to wring out the truth that she herself believes. But when this does not happen, she questions us for more enlightenment or to discover if she has taken down the thought correctly.

"There is honesty in her approach, for this way we can give our attention to the normal questions which might arise when the reader goes through this book. We think the book becomes more trustworthy this way. Perhaps the reader wants more proof of this writer's work. Does she really write what we are saying? This is the natural question, we think. But there is no way we can prove our position. No, we cannot prove any theory, for there is this invisibility, you see. When the ones in earth life learn to line up their good truth with the truth of God, they might be able to have our understanding. Proof—we will work on this, of course, but we do not know how as yet."

The next day the message became personal again, just as it was at the beginning of this chapter. The Brother who specializes in this correspondence, the one who has the power of transmission, spoke. "The open channel will be our best means of grasping the truth that God-mind has to give. This God-mind takes the truth that is everlasting, that is the truth that empties itself with no thought of ego, the truth that brings us to the understanding of the oneness with God. Gentle breezes that flow toward your mind give this truth to you. This truth does not come by any hard means. There is no agony of mind, nor any thought that this truth comes through the mind that is emptied so that spiritual entities enter you to take over. There is no one taking over your mind, is there?"

I agreed. I am always in calm control, else how could I question, how could I doubt, how could I seek further enlightenment?

"There is no thought of the truth that comes to you being other than helpful, is there?"

Again the answer is "no." The material that comes to me brightens my life in every respect.

"This truth opens your mind to new perspectives, doesn't it?"

Yes, I certainly do have new perspectives that reach far beyond what I ever considered before I received this truth. The perspective of reincarnation is enough to widen my horizon, to give me new considerations concerning who I am, to help me find meaning and purpose in my life.

"There is the thought entity—you—who gives herself to this writing in order to keep her life in the pattern she came with." With this final statement about me, my communicator turned again to the reader.

"This is our truth we bring to this book. This communication, though it takes time, takes less time than the time-consuming worries and tensions that take the energy that steals the body's reserve strength, that depletes the inner forces. This time-consuming manner takes far more time than the time spent here on communication. This touch will prosper you right away, take you to your greatest strength—God. This truth center, this Brotherhood, this Counselor, this Christ-promised teacher/counselor, this team of those devoted to the giving of this help, take this moment to offer you their touch, their help, their teamwork to make your life prosper.

"There is no way to teach you all to do this communication as in a class. This business of connecting you to our true tone is the individual touch we give. This touch must be done person to person, not class to teacher or teacher to class. Give yourself in person to this communication."

Whenever someone asks me how this material comes to me, I try, but never succeed, to give a satisfactory explanation. I know how it feels to me, and now I know the explanation the Brotherhood gives. Still.... like this Counselor/Teacher/Brotherhood says, the only way to find out is to try it yourself.

CHAPTER 14

TEAMING UP WITH THE BROTHERHOOD

What must I do to receive and keep God-mind truth?

"We greet you, the reader, with a paternal salute," one of the Brotherhood began. "We want to enter into your experience, into your central core, your reality. But we cannot enter to give our help unless you take us at our word."

Trust, the key word implied in all the Brotherhood says, holds the key to a successful relationship between us and our Counselor. Again and again they state our responsibility in attaining the help we want. *We must initiate the request.* Not just once, you understand, but each time you and I want help, we must ask for it. No doubt the request activates the trust factor which in turn awakens the energy of the universe on our behalf.

"There must be permission for the door to open," this same Brother affirms. "Nobody can impose himself upon you without your permission. To open the door, the thought must be sent out that the Brotherhood may enter. Then we come in."

To become part of what my communicator calls "the time/space project," we must do three things: first, give permission for the Brotherhood to enter; second, present an open mind to them; third, in your inner temple hold the thought that the Brotherhood is present. "Then you will be ready to receive, and you will," is the assurance.

Concerning the three steps in getting help, my advanced teacher has this to say. "If it seems overly simplified, it is because you must not understand the power of thought. *Thought* is the power of the universe. Thought gives the impetus to the teamwork between us. Thought transfers its generous gift of power into the work that the writer and we do together here in this book. The thought we give out will reach the thought reaching toward it to make the contact we need to talk to one another. When these two thoughts meet, communication takes place.

"You must understand that to attain the truth from God-mind, we form the open channel through which the connection is entered. This channel of truth empties itself of all ego, all temporal thought of gain or power, and it presents the true, pure truth of God. Truth for the sake of truth, that is what is needed here by those who want to be receivers. The channel gives the purity of truth, the wonderful revelations, the perfection that is the truth for that person."

Communication as described above is remarkable, but unless we take the truth from God-mind and interweave it into our inner selves, we have little in the way of permanent value. People whom I have told about this God-mind truth think it fascinating that I can get this material in the way I do. They are, in fact, carried away by the communication itself. As for the message, they think it very interesting, even beautiful. However, until they make contact with the Brotherhood on their own and develop a two-way communication that leads them to connect with the open channel, the words remain extraordinary but impersonal.

"It takes much effort," my communicator states, "to enter the truth into your consciousness, for the earth-mind is strong, and you probably are filled with much that comes from that mind. God-mind truth will create wonder and doubt within you; therefore, you must work hard to overcome skepticism. When you consider what is involved in the total acceptance of God-mind truth, you may fall away.

"The God-mind truth gives you much to harvest, but there is much to weed out before the harvest. Therefore, take warning that this God-mind truth will take you to another truth, to another understanding. Take the warning seriously, for you may not wish to have your truth taken to the open channel where it will be changed forever.

"Once you accept this truth we speak of, it will become personal. Then you will be the new truth in expression. This touch we give you realigns your truth concepts so that your entire understanding is recreated. There is no such thing as 'a little truth.' Therefore, take this matter of truth seriously, not lightly."

From the beginning of the book to the end, those in the Brotherhood have insisted that it takes no special talent to team up with them. If you need proof, I am that proof, for I haven't a mystical bone in my body. I have never been part of a seance, nor have I ever entered a trance, not that I condemn either one. "The Brotherhood works with all who seek us," came the assurance. "We want you to come and to put the truth that we talk about on your list of most-wanted items. This truth, however consuming, will be that which brings you the complete freedom we all must have to evolve into the wonderful entities we wish to be."

To be the very best receiver possible, these advanced spirits list several things we can do. First and foremost, tell the truth to them. Telling the truth may seem like an obvious thing to do considering they can read our thoughts. But telling the truth involves openness between us and the Brotherhood. "To be honest," one spirit declares, "you must say up front what it is you want to get from this relationship. Be honest in noting each desire, each question, each good or bad thought. Be open with yourself.

"You may feel antagonism if you find this truth hard to accept. Then say so. Give us the chance to comment on this too. *Nothing that you think is important will be tossed aside by us.* The truth that will come to you in response to your statements and questions will be to help you work out your life."

In the beginning of my relationship with the Brotherhood, I wondered just how much truth I had a right to expect. Some days I received pages and pages of material. Was I being selfish? How much is enough?

"There is no amount of truth that is right for a certain

person. It just comes indefinitely to you." Apparently I was not asking for more than I should ask. "Never will the truth of God-mind run out," my communicator assures me. "The truth of God is entered into the universe, into the vastness of that which entities call the powerful terrestrial outreaches. In the earth plane people believe that everything is limited, but God is unlimited.

"This relationship between us will give your life stability. It will give your life its anchor. The Brotherhood want to give this truth to you and even more as you can receive it and handle it. There is no limit, remember. There is no time limit nor is there a limit on the amount of truth there is. Take all you want. What questions do you have about your life? Relationships? Guidance in decisions? Whom to marry? The trust that you will develop in this truth will guide you in even more and greater questions.

"As for speaking to spirits, do not even consider the possibility that our relationship is anything except God-inspired. There is spirit and there is body. The spirit, the reality of the personality, takes its truth from spirit. The body must take its truth from the earth-mind. But who is in control here? The spirit or the body? The spirit, of course. The spirit is the dominant one within this body, not the heart, the liver, the bladder. These organs merely exist to help the body function. They do not take the power of control over the body. Nobody rules your own body except you. Then it is spirit that does the ruling, is it not? Then the spirit must get truth that will prosper it from spirit. *Therefore, to talk spirit to spirit is to qualify in the realm of the great, not the realm of the foolish.*

"This unseen world, this second plane of life, is real. It has permanence. But what in the earth plane is permanent? Nothing! Therefore, do not fear what is spirit. Fear that which is material, for it has no truth to sustain it. The earth plane produces growth that takes its truth from the impermanent. Therefore, the impermanent will fade away, become obsolete, turn itself into valueless energy. But that which is spirit will be the substance that energizes each thought, each concept, each entity with that which is permanent."

On this note my communicator completed the first part of

this chapter. The next day they signed in with the usual, "This is the Brotherhood of God here," and plunged ahead to say, "Today we will give the rest of the material for this chapter. Take this down: This Brotherhood gives itself to the work that is of God-mind. We, who are energized and teamed up with Christ, have our own place in taking the truth of the God of the Universe to those of you who request it. There is no truth in your experience that will give you what you need as will this truth from God-mind. Then why do you hesitate? Take this offer now. Take this truth we give you."

Together we can accomplish anything! How many times have you and I heard and said this statement of positive hope? The Brotherhood, however, extends this statement: "Men and women with God's truth within them will take on the most horrendous tasks with confidence." The first statement reflects earth-mind thinking. The second, of course, reflects God-mind truth. Apparently there is a spiritual law at work here. Those advanced spirits say there is no way to go against the law that says, "when we become a truth-centered entity, we take what we need and want and live in perfect freedom." And this is another way of saying that we can, indeed, accomplish anything—when we unite with God-mind truth.

How many of us believe that we can accomplish anything we want? One Brother says that only a few believe this. "They enter this truth with misgivings. They work to earn money, they say. They work, they take, they band together with others to get what they want. But to reach out into the universe, believing in this creative substance that will take its form from your thought, your belief in it—well, that is rather much to accept. They work on in ignorance of what any entity can accomplish with his spiritual powers. They work because they see only earth results with their eyes. But they could see spiritual results with their eyes, too, if they would manifest as they are able."

I told my communicator that I must be one of those they described—one who cannot believe with confidence. However, I stated my deep desire in life, and I ended by asking how I can manifest this desire.

The Brotherhood/Counselor, who welcomes my doubts as

well as my uncertainties, commented. "This desire you have expressed here is in your inner temple, and you will manifest this desire or whatever you think is important. This thought will persist into reality, not into indebtedness, but into debt free results. Watch it carefully and see what happens!" My desire was for a word processor, and the next day I had an offer of a word processor to use temporarily.

"Nothing you want may be denied if it is for your good," the messenger continued. "This good thought will grow into reality fast or slowly depending on your belief in its importance. Results come when a person needs this thing. Nothing that enters your God-self will be the truth inverted. Nothing that enters your God-self will be bad. This is our promise here—this is our truth. The Brotherhood watches over those who commit their lives to the God of the Universe, to the ones who seek help even though they hold a small concept of God.

"We do not measure the degree of your faith. We do not give help only to 'worthy' people. We give help to all who open their minds to this possibility. This God of the Universe is not jealous. He does not insist that you approach Him in only the one or two methods that religion outlines. There need be no trials or suffering. God does not cause negative things to happen in life; He opens everyone's eyes to the easy way, to the wonderful way of life."

These advanced spirits promise to take our temperaments into consideration in the matter of giving us truth. None of us, according to this Counselor, can handle the entire truth all at one time. "This truth must be portioned out so that you may grow in stages, step by step," the messenger explains. "This truth is powerful, but it is not dangerous. The only reason for going to it bit by bit is to help you to absorb it all and take it to your lifetime experience."

I inquired if this truth from God-mind goes to entities in the next plane of life. "This is possible, of course," my source responded. "It is possible and it happens, but there is no way entities here can trust this truth except by entering earth life with it. The truth cannot be tested here and must be taken at face value. The best plan, we think, is to learn truth while you are in earth life. Then you can practice it in the living of your life."

I suggested that we examine more closely this truth about manifesting desires and needs from God's substance. I asked if someone in the Brotherhood would tell us of people who, in this earth life, used this truth to manifest their needs and their desires. Here is the reply.

"There is this entity here who took this truth into his lifetime. He made use of it whenever he had a need or a right desire. This Brother manifested his own truth in the form of material goods. The thought projected into form for him because he entered earth life believing in this possibility."

I inquired if there are people in the earth plane now who manifest their needs and desires in the way they outlined—by the substance of God used to manifest thoughts. Here is the interesting and graphic reply.

"In the earth plane teachers who take this message seriously take their thoughts into manifestation. They simply enter the thought of this manifestation in the temple of their true self, the God-self. Then they realize the thought that enters this holy place. 'There it is,' they say to the God of the Universe. 'Be teamed up with me in this manifestation.' Then they turn their minds to the thought in its completed form. There it is! There it manifests.

"These teachers take their own entities to this plane now and then to enter our Brotherhood to take the wetness out of their thinking. This wetness comes when they become too involved in the earth-mind. They must 'dry out' so to speak. The earth-mind wets or dampens the greatness that God-mind produces. The wetness gives us the image here of taking the bright shining ideas and teeming them into mush, into the non-creative thought form. *Teeming* means the humid condition that is unable to project pure thought. The wetness takes a bright form that exists in mind, that enters the entity's consciousness, that unites with the Brotherhood to give the great gift of substance, and it wets it down into the mush we spoke of."

My communicator spoke of teachers who manifest their

thoughts. What of the other people—people like the reader and me? The reply pointed out that "the ones who manifest these things that they need and that they want take their own thoughts into manifestation, but they do not take this thought to others. They would be willing, but there is no one to heed their thought. The manifestation is not easy to accept, but it is easy to do.

"Realize that truth is like the tender touch of a plant that gently brushes against your leg or your hand. Tender young plants must get attention and nourishment to become the big plants that will give shade or which will bloom. This same plant that brushes against you will wither and die if you take it to the truth of earth-mind that says the plant is a weed. You will reject it, you see. The plant will go to the earth again with no truth coming forth.

"No one will be into this truth more than will those of you who read this book. Some may read it to ridicule, or to laugh, or to wonder, or even to give derision. But those of you who bring your God-selves to this truth will benefit greatly. Those who think the book is full of nonsense will turn away from God-mind. They will take more of this truth to mind, however, than they expect. There is always enlightenment when the God-mind truth touches a person's mind.

"Believers who try to read this book in order to put themselves in tune with the God of the Universe will connect with the truth of God-mind. Then they will prosper beyond belief. They will come forth through the half-truths, through the earth-mind truth that tries to enfold them in its web. They will enter into this truth concept to become one with God, and they will advance, grow, and become that which they want to be.

"There is wonderful news in this book that can free people from their own entrapment in the earth life. They want greater freedom, and they want wonderful truth. This God-mind truth tempers the whole business of earth life with the wisdom that is eternal. A gentle thought enters to improve each day for you. Yes, this truth speaks to the pure hope within you that you are everlasting. We speak to that spark which is your divinity, that spark that gets its glow from the

God of the Universe, that spark that results from the growth of your spirit in lifetime after lifetime".

Beautiful and apt metaphors enrich the messages that the Brothers bring to this book through God-mind. One of these uses two of the seasons, spring and winter, to explain yet again how earth-mind and God-mind function in our lives.

"Winter closes the soul, but spring offers it hope again. Winter is the earth-mind that pours its truth, half-truth and untruth upon each earth-life person. Spring is the new God-mind truth that reawakens you from the long winter of unhappiness or dissatisfaction. This God-mind truth teams up with the Brotherhood to present itself to each one who asks. Then spring will come to that person with a new hope and a new manifestation. There never need be this winter of the soul again. It will end permanently once the entity joins up with God-mind."

Whether all people hear the truth or not, these in the Brotherhood assure us that the truth remains the truth. "The principle of God—the truth—is unchanging. This principle, this God of the Universe, this truth that seeks its own, will be here for each of you who want it. It is your hope for a better world and for better soul growth."

Concern exists among the Brotherhood that many people are reluctant to turn away from earth-mind. They wonder why any of us would hesitate to accept their offer of help in making this God connection. One asks, "Why would you even need to think this over?"

One Brother lists possible reasons for our hesitation. For example, mention is made of the churches that claim truth must come from their pulpits, from their own religious concepts. "If you, reader, belong to any group which lays claim to the entire truth, take warning. There is no limit on God. There is no possible way to limit God's truth by passing church laws or setting up doctrines.

"The God of the Universe takes His truth to whomever He wants wherever He wants whenever He wants. He tells His truth through those who speak to this writer. He tells His truth to those who tune in to God-mind, and He will not be held in check by any priest or teacher or minister. He overrides the truth of those churches to present His own truth for each person.

"There is no way to take you to the mountain top of the experience of being one with God. Where would we go? The experience that comes to those who become one with God is unique. That is the truth. There is no experience of one person that can be applied to another. That is how individual we all are.

"Because of our uniqueness there can be no truth spread out like grass seed. This truth must be planted in the soft earth which is you. The seed must be suited to your soil, to your understanding. Truth that is your own must be given to you personally. That is what is meant by having this personal relationship with God. This oneness with God is only in the person, never the group happening.

"There is nothing in the Universe that will be denied to those who are one with God. They have the freedom of space travel, the freedom to walk the earth if they wish, the freedom to be the entities that sing, dance, become masters of the arts. They tell others that they have never known this absolute freedom before. They compare it to the wider understanding or to the uniting with universal substance that pours through them on command.

"They tell us they reach the ultimate in every experience, in each endeavor. They never resist this oneness with God. They reach higher and higher in expression to be those who excel in the wonderful expressions that this oneness can bring."

Finally, my communicator says that there are no adequate words to describe this oneness with God. How can words convey to me or to you what we have not experienced? They insist that whether we know it or not, we want to be one with God because we are, after all, offshoots of God who must return to Him. "Nothing we do now will take this concept any further," this Brother/Counselor says finally. "There is the truth, there is the reader, and there is this Brotherhood waiting to help unite you with your true identity, the one with God."

Books and Products to help establish
The Global Spiritual Awakening

Jean Foster is an important new writer, a very clear channel and one of the many now appearing to show the way to the New Age. She has already completed two more books that continue the revelation of truth that is her mission. These books, "The Truth That Goes Unclaimed" and " Eternal Gold" are expected to be in print in 1987.

In the meantime, we at Uni★Sun will do our best to publish books and offer products that make a real contribution to the global spiritual awakening that has already begun on this planet. For a free copy of our catalogue, please write to:

Uni★Sun
P. O. Box 25421
Kansas City, Missouri 64119
U.S.A.